SHARING YOUR STORY

Recording Life's Details with Mini Books

by Ali Edwards

IT'S ALL GOOD

WHEN I FIRST LAID EYES ON THE PROJECTS in this book, I immediately thought two things:

1. There's no one I'd rather have teach me about mini books than Ali Edwards.
2. I want to make one right now!

Why would I want to learn from Ali? Besides the fact that her "keep it simple" mentality and teaching style tend to melt stress away, replacing it with enthusiasm, she's the master of spinning stories and photos into works of art. So I can't think of anyone better to simplify the memory-recording process into beautiful, mini pieces of art with no limits and no deadlines. I love my chronological scrapbooks, but let's face it—they only technically "end" when we quit making memories, and that's, well, never.

Ali reminds us that a mini book is the perfect "anytime" project for any theme, whether it's a storybook presentation of a child's sports photos, a recipe album or a useful travel album to track not only vacation photos, but maps, favorite landmarks and lists of off-the-beaten-path cafés and markets as well.

In this book, Ali and her team of amazing scrapbookers demonstrate that mini books can be added to little by little, or they can be completed in a month, a week or even a day. The projects in this book are so inspiring, I'm going to keep several on my craft table to work on, just to delight in the process (that is, if my toddler doesn't find the "Thomas the Train"—themed mini book before it's completed). When I finish one, I'll just start another. None of the stress but all of the fun and creativity.

So now I'm off to start another mini book. I may finish today and I may not, but as Ali says, "It's all good."

Britney Mellen

CONTENTS

WHY LITTLE BOOKS?

I CAN'T REMEMBER EXACTLY WHAT INSPIRED me to make my first mini book. But I specifically remember what I felt when I looked down at my completed project: a sense of accomplishment and excitement. Accomplishment because in my hands I held a finished project with a beginning, middle and end, and excitement because I could tell this was a format I was going to want to use again and again.

And again and again.

To me, mini books are freedom. They are confidence-builders. They are fun. They are a break from the process of scrapbooking in your regular format.

Many of the minis featured in this book are ongoing—meaning they're works-in-progress, created to document and record moments or events as they're experienced. The idea is to put together the foundation of the book and fill it in with content as you go about your life. This is part of the process of living creatively.

One of my favorite things about minis is that they tend to fit within your own two hands. They feel alive. Often there are no page protectors, so you can literally feel the textures of the accents and the photos and the written words. My books have been touched by many hands—the pages turned and the words read. Little fingerprints dot the photos. This is part of the beauty for me—that people are actively experiencing these books.

Another aspect of minis that I love is that they continually challenge me creatively. The small size makes trying something new and different a little easier to swallow. I enjoy experimenting with a variety of materials, such as fabric, wood and plastic, and coming up with unique ways to tell a story.

As you page through this book (created with the help of a fabulous team of designers!),

I hope you encounter concepts that make you feel like getting up and creating and documenting your life. With every album, we share different ideas and themes that may work for you as well. I also invite you to take a risk and try something outside of your comfort zone. Those are the moments when we tend to grow the most. Use the projects for inspiration and see where they take you. (And if you have any basic questions about types of mini books or how to make one from scratch, check out the reference section at the back of the book.)

Most of all, enjoy. We hope you find the same delight in the process of creating minis as we do!

A. Edwards

chapter 1

Record-Keeping

WE ALL HAVE THINGS IN OUR LIVES THAT ARE WORTH DOCUMENTING. Some of them are story-based, and others are more basic, like daily notes, a list of favorite TV shows or family recipes. This is one of my favorite themes: the story of our everyday existence. The minutes and moments that make up the bulk of our lives.

To me, these are the things that make life interesting. The bits of this and that—the things we often overlook or throw away. In reality, these are the details that tell what our real lives are like—our daily routines, going to the store with a list (or PDA!) in hand, our favorite foods, how we like to relax. These are the things I wish I knew about my relatives.

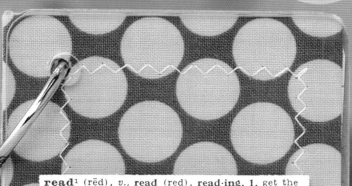

DOCUMENT YOUR FAVORITE BOOKS

This is a fun little 3" x 5" album I created to document my favorite books from yesterday and today. Using library cards for my notes and scans of book covers from the Internet (you can also photograph or scan your book covers), I created an album that's easy to update as I read more books.

Try This!

Use this mini for documenting:

· Favorite outfits for quick reference

· Favorite movies

· Quotes

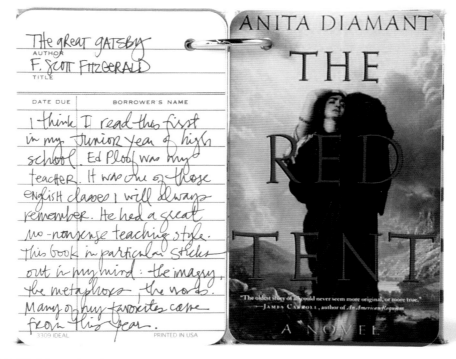

AUTHOR

TITLE

DATE DUE   BORROWER'S NAME

READ

these days I record books I am reading online at a site: www.goodreads.com

I love to read. It has been that way for as long as I can remember. I read all sorts of books ~ fiction, non-fiction, how-to, picture, art, etc. They all teach me one thing or another. Sometimes I will read non-stop. Voraciously. The sort of reading where it is almost painful to stop. Where it feels as if you are living within the story, where it has become a part of you. Other times I will only read here and there, mostly at night before bed. At all times I am a collector. Hunting and gathering stories to read, lessons to learn, art to experiment. This is a life-long thing. A huge part of who I am. I love to live with books.

DOCUMENT AR 2006

The GREAT GATSBY

AUTHOR

F. SCOTT FITZGERALD

TITLE

DATE DUE   BORROWER'S NAME

I think I read this first in my Junior year of high school. Ed Ploof was my teacher. It was one of those english classes I will always remember. He had a great no-nonsense teaching style. This book in particular sticks out in my mind: the imagry, the metaphors, the words. Many of my favorites came from this year.

3309 IDEAL   PRINTED IN USA

ANITA DIAMANT

THE RED TENT

"The oldest story of all could never seem more original, or more true."
—JAMES CARROLL, author of *An American Requiem*

A NOVEL

BOOKS *by Ali Edwards.*

Supplies *Album:* D. Reeves Design House; *Mini tag:* American Tag Company; *Corner rounder:* Marvy Uchida; *Stamps:* Educational Insights; *Ink:* StazOn, Tsukineko; *Fabric:* Amy Butler; *Rub-ons:* Making Memories and American Crafts; *Circle epoxy sticker:* Love, Elsie for KI Memories; *Pen:* American Crafts; *Other:* Library cards, binder ring and thread.

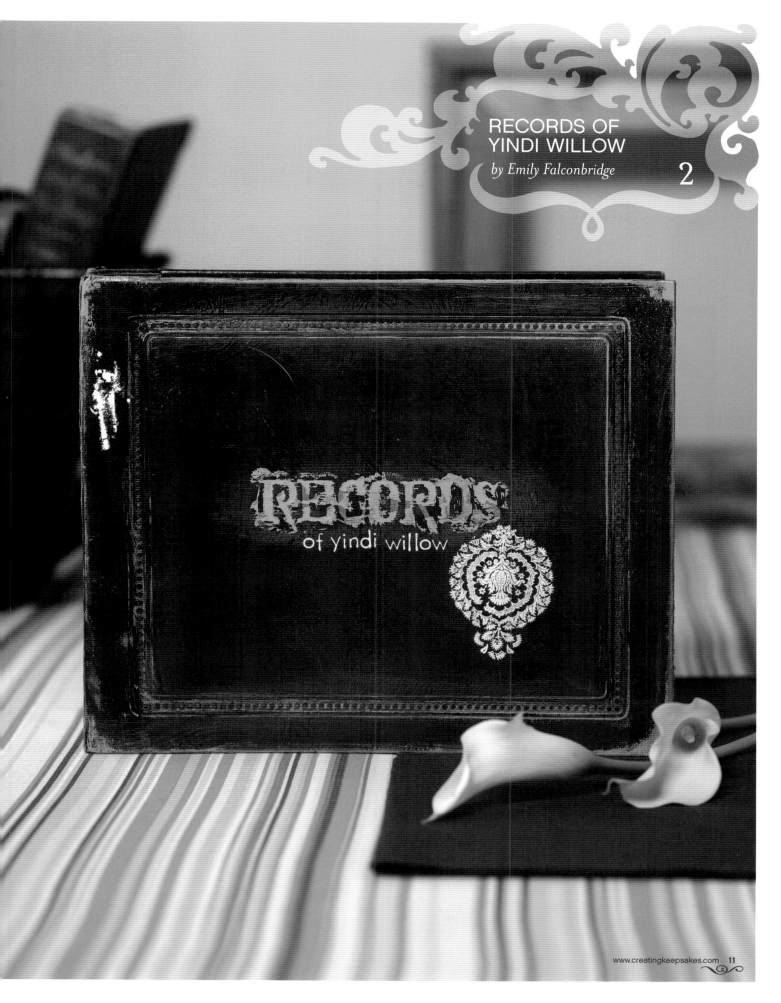

Use this mini for recording:

- Scores from family game nights
- Gardening and planting schedules
- Daily experiences on a vacation

KEEP A DAILY LOG

Emily found this old 7½" x 9" album for storing vinyl records in a thrift store and thought it would make a perfect daily log. In the left-hand pockets, she tucked a new kind of record—journaling about the day—and in the facing pockets, she included a photo.

Think of other types of books or albums you can repurpose to create a similar daily record. Perhaps you can tuck your journaling and photo into a modern version of the vinyl record holder—a CD case. Or create a similar album using tags or CD sleeves and simply cut an opening to frame your photo.

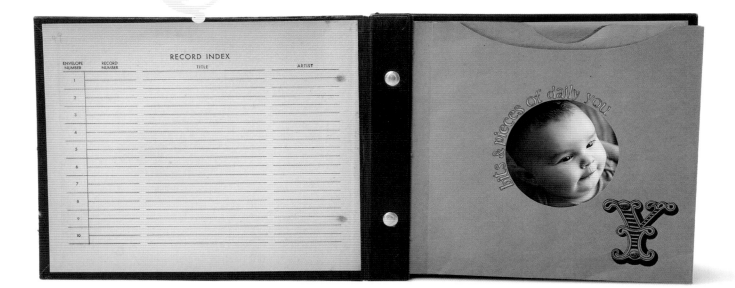

RECORDS OF YINDI WILLOW *by Emily Falconbridge.*
Supplies *Paint:* Matisse Derivan; *Other:* Vintage vinyl record album.

This is me.

RECORD IMPORTANT INFORMATION ABOUT A CHILD FOR A CAREGIVER OR TEACHER

This is a very special 5½" x 8½" book—I created it as a tool for my son's teachers and caregivers. It's an introduction to my son—his likes, dislikes, etc.—and will hopefully help them communicate with each other more effectively.

To create a similar album, make a base design and follow it on each page. For my album, I created a template in a page-layout program (I use Adobe InDesign), which makes it easy to update later when the content changes. My template includes a dotted box frame for each photo and a journaling box.

THIS IS ME *by Ali Edwards.*
Supplies *Album:* D. Reeves Design House; *Cardstock:* Bazzill Basics Paper; *Patterned paper:* Anna Griffin and American Crafts; *Circle accents:* KI Memories; *Square punch:* McGill; *Font:* Garamond, Internet.

I learn best with pictures and
one-on-one instructions. I love to look
at books and am starting to read.
I love letters and numbers.
Sometimes I need help following
directions with reminders or
redirection if I get distracted.
I especially like to know what is going
to happen next.

These are a few of my favorite things:
swimming, watching movies, visiting
Grandma & Grandpa at the beach,
eating pizza and/or ice cream, sledding,
recess, Star Wars, playing chase,
drinking OJ, tickle-time, McDonald's,
leaving my socks on when I go to sleep,
going on airplanes *and* other
interesting adventures.

MUSIC
by Dedra Long

4

wish i could 4.18
sinkin' soon 4.38
the sun doesn't like you 2.59
until the end 3.56
not my friend 2.54
thinking about you 3.17
broken 3.19
my dear country 3.25
wake me up 2.46
be my somebody 3.36
little room 2.43
rosie's lullaby 3.56
not too late 3.30

"thinking about you" music video
"until the end" music video

MUSIC

Dedra created this 8" x 8" mini book to document her favorite music and CD artwork. "We usually buy our music on iTunes now," she explains. "And while that's convenient, I miss buying CDs! The cover artwork and inserts inspire me—they're mini works of art." On every tag in the album, next to each band, group or artist, Dedra wrote the reason she loves the music or the feelings it evokes in her.

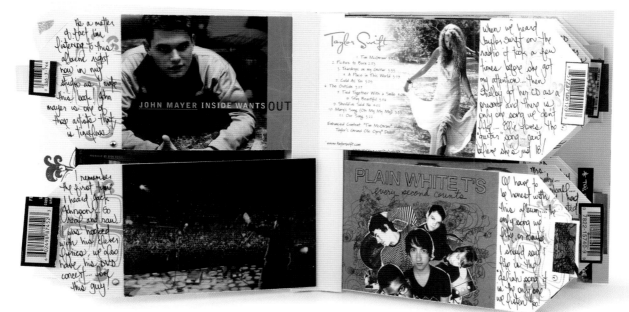

MUSIC *by Dedra Long.*

Supplies *Album:* Mema Designs; *Patterned paper:* Creative Imaginations and Anna Griffin; *Transparency:* Hambly Studios; *Chipboard letters:* Heidi Swapp for Advantus; *Chipboard swirls:* Maya Road; *Glitter:* Stickles, Ranger Industries; *Bookplate:* BasicGrey; *Stamps:* Orange Bus Studios, 7gypsies and Catslife Press; *Brad:* Making Memories; *Other:* Staples and jewels. ·

5   EAT
    by Laura Kurz

CREATE A MONTHLY MEAL PLANNER

While minis are great for recording the past, they're also useful for planning ahead and recording your life-in-progress. A meal planner is the perfect combination of both—you're using the planner now, and you're also documenting what your family loves to eat (or how you would like them to eat!).

Laura created this 9" x 6½" mini planner to help her stay organized and prepare some meal ideas in advance. She created a separate card for each month of the year, using the back of the card to add menu suggestions for the weeks in the month. When she finds a recipe she wants to try, she simply clips it to the month she intends to use it.

EAT by Laura Kurz.

Supplies *Folder:* 7gypsies; *Cardstock:* American Crafts; *Chipboard letters and day-of-the-week stickers:* Heidi Swapp for Advantus; *Rub-on scroll accent:* Maya Road; *Letter stickers:* Doodlebug Design, SEI and American Crafts; *Other:* Clip.

SUNDAY	MONDAY	SUNDAY	MONDAY
chicken dijon Rice (chicken + broccoli) broccoli	pasta w/ mushrooms salad	broccoli stuffed chicken Rice	mushroom Ravioli salad

TUESDAY	WEDNESDAY	TUESDAY	WEDNESDAY
broccoli + cheese quiche salad	grilled cheese soup salad	Raspberry chicken corn Rolls	salmon w/ soy sauce Rice asparagus

THURSDAY	FRIDAY	THURSDAY	FRIDAY
meatloaf au gratin potatoes Rice	Restaurant or pizza	pasta w/ mushrooms salad	Restaurant or pizza

GIFT GUIDE
by Laura Kurz

6

0 1 2
3 4 5
6 7 8

gift guidE

DESIGN A GIFT GUIDE TO PLAN
AHEAD FOR SPECIAL OCCASIONS

Never be unprepared for a birthday or anniversary again! With a gift guide, you can record important details, like dates, gift ideas and more! Laura created a 6" x 2⅕" gift-guide format that's easy to follow. She used the same formula on each page: a picture of someone who's having a birthday that month, a list of birthdays and anniversaries, and gift ideas.

Try This!

Use this mini for documenting:

- Important dates in a school schedule
- Reminders for regular bill payments
- A child's activities and hobbies

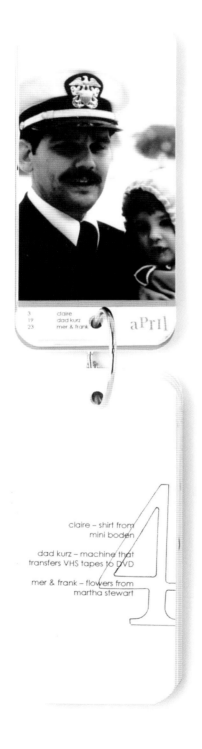

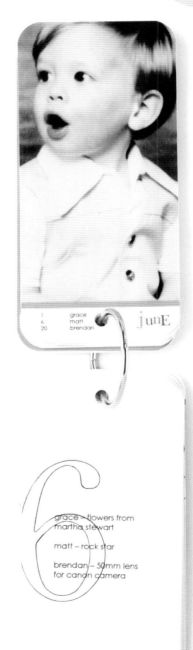

3	claire
19	dad kurz
23	mer & frank

aPril

1	grace
6	matt
20	brendan

junE

claire – shirt from mini boden

dad kurz – machine that transfers VHS tapes to DVD

mer & frank – flowers from martha stewart

grace – flowers from martha stewart

matt – rock star

brendan – 50mm lens for canon camera

GIFT GUIDE *by Laura Kurz*

Supplies *Cardstock:* Bazzill Basics Paper and American Crafts; *Corner rounder:* Marvy Uchida; *Chipboard numbers:* BasicGrey; *Rub-on letters:* Heidi Grace Designs; *Pen:* American Crafts; *Font:* Century Gothic, Microsoft; *Other:* Binder ring.

PHOTO LOG

7

by Mou Saha

KEEP TRACK OF THE PHOTOS YOU TAKE

Whether you're a budding writer, artist or photographer, a mini is a great place to keep a record of the work you're creating because you can take it with you for on-the-spot record-keeping. Mou created this 4" x 4" album to serve as a photography workbook as she experiments with her new camera. You can use stamps, blank labels or journaling cards to fill in the details you want to remember.

Try This!

Use this mini for documenting:

- Gardening schedules/progress
- Freelance work accepted/pending payment
- Books you've read

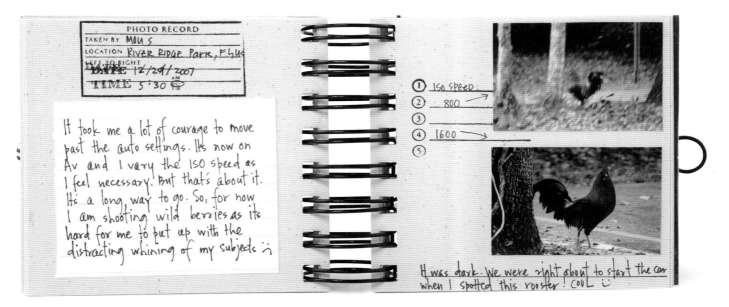

PHOTO LOG *by Mou Saha*

Supplies *Spiral-bound album:* Rusty Pickle; *Letter stickers:* Heidi Swapp for Advantus; *Cardstock stickers, gaffer tape, elastic band, and date and time stamps:* 7gypsies; *Stamps:* Autumn Leaves and FontWerks; *Ink:* Ranger Industries (red) and Tsukineko (black); *Index cards:* Oxford; *Pen:* Marvy Uchida; *Bead and floss:* Michaels.

BEST FRIEND

8

by Laura Kurz

CHARMER

best friend
08

We all receive important paperwork that we file away, but with documents you'll likely refer to on a regular basis, such as records from the veterinarian, you may consider transforming your file into a practical, self-contained album.

Because most of this type of paperwork is usually at least 8½" x 11", Laura created a 9" x 12" book by modifying a standard filing envelope and converting it into a three-ring book. She altered the cover with cardstock, then punched holes in it. She also created an envelope on the inside front cover to hold receipts, prescriptions and other important reminders. "I really want to keep my dog's health records in one place, especially since she's getting older and is having more health issues," Laura explains.

Try This!

Use this mini for documenting:
- Bills
- Household repairs
- Car maintenance

BEST FRIEND *by Laura Kurz*

Supplies *Cardstock and photo corners:* American Crafts; *"Best Friend" stamp:* Autumn Leaves; *Number stickers:* Doodlebug Design and Heidi Swapp for Advantus; *Bone clip:* Carolee's Creations; *Other:* Binder rings.

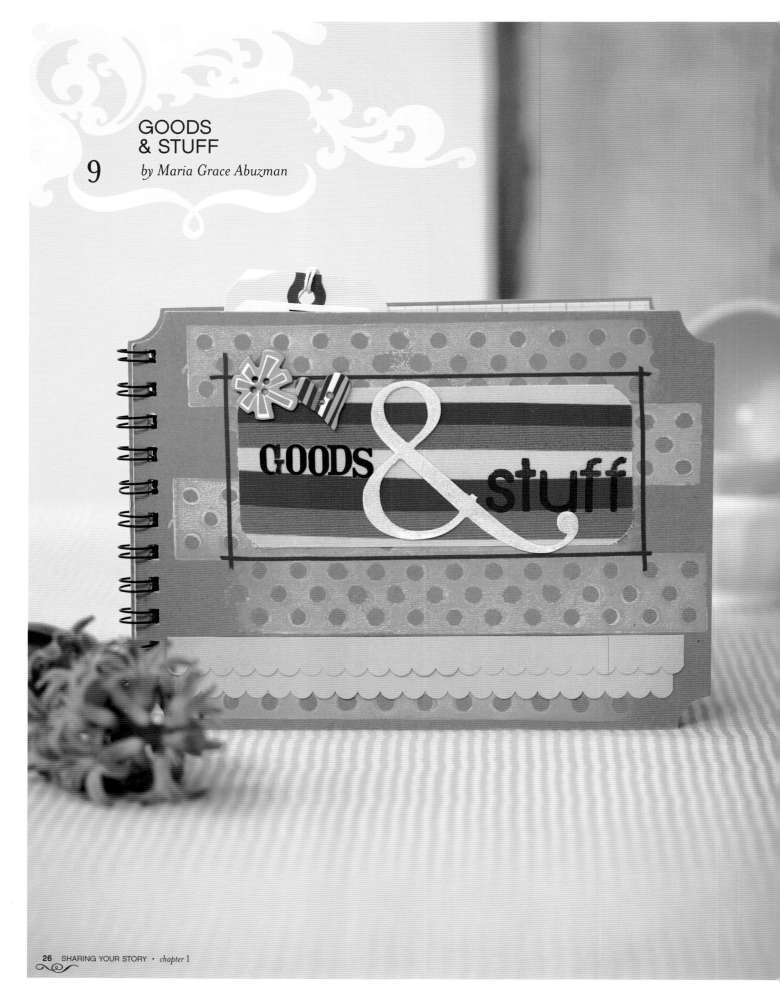

GOODS & STUFF

9 *by Maria Grace Abuzman*

CREATE A PERSONAL DIRECTORY OF FAVORITES

Maria Grace has friends from other states and countries who visit and want to know her recommendations for great places to shop. So she created this 6" x 8" album of her personal favorites, with all the pertinent information (addresses, phone numbers, contact names), along with her impressions. "You can think of this album as a very personal, very subject-specific tour book," she says.

"If I wanted to place this album in a location of my house for decoration, I would use muted colors to match my furniture," she explains. "If I lent this album to a friend, I'd include extra pages for her to create her own entries."

Try This!

Use this mini for documenting:

- Favorite restaurants
- Family-friendly entertainment choices
- Date-night activities

GOODS & STUFF *by Maria Grace Abuzman*

Supplies *Software:* Adobe Illustrator, Adobe Systems; *Cardstock:* Paper Source and Creative Imaginations; *Patterned paper:* Scenic Route; *Fabric paper and chipboard embellishments:* KI Memories; *Rub-ons:* American Crafts; *Stickers:* Creative Imaginations, Chronicle Books, Heidi Grace Designs and FontWerks; *Stamps:* FontWerks, Jenni Bowlin Studio and Rubber Soul; *Ink:* Ranger Industries and Tsukineko; *Foam stamps:* Not Your Ordinary Foam Stamp Set, Kit of the Month, *Creating Keepsakes; Paint:* Blick; *Border strip and glitter:* Doodlebug Design; *Die-cut machine:* QuicKutz; *Binding:* Zutter Innovative Products; *Notch tool and corner rounder:* Fiskars; *Fonts:* Fling, www.myfonts.com; Last Words, www.fontco.com; *Other:* Graphic tape, mailing tags and photo corners.

WATCH ME
GROW

10 *by Maggie Holmes*

RECORD A BABY'S FIRST FEW DAYS AND MONTHS

Maggie designed this 8" x 8" book as a place to keep an ongoing record of her baby as she grows. Says Maggie, "I wanted a format that would be easy to add to as time goes on and that would allow me to insert any number of photos, journaling pages, etc. I also wanted to be able to use a variety of sizes, and this format is perfect for that."

Maggie used Plexiglas for the covers and some of the pages, and inserted photo and transparency pages into the book by punching holes in them with a hole punch. She used binder rings to hold it all together.

Try This!

Use this mini for documenting:

- A new pet
- A child's firsts
- Things you're learning at a new job

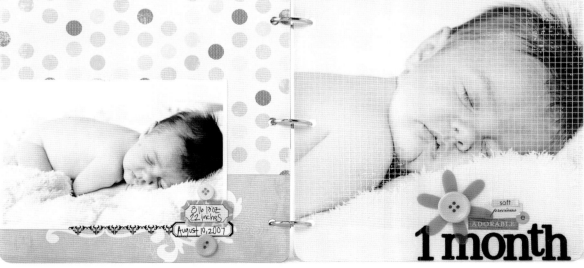

WATCH ME GROW *by Maggie Holmes.*

Supplies *Album:* D. Reeves Design House; *Patterned paper:* Making Memories; *Rub-ons:* KI Memories, Autumn Leaves, BasicGrey, American Crafts and Hambly Studios; *Transparency:* Hambly Studios; *Gaffer tape:* 7gypsies; *Labels:* Li'l Davis Designs, Martha Stewart Crafts and Chronicle Books; *Letter stickers, metal tab, buttons and stickers:* Making Memories; *Acrylic shape:* Heidi Swapp for Advantus; *Stamp:* Catslife Press; *Hole punch:* Fiskars; *Pen:* Zig Millennium, EK Success.

RECORD THE DETAILS THAT ARE ESSENTIAL TO A HAPPY LIFE

When we get caught up in the daily grind, it's nice to have reminders of what's really important to us—the things that truly matter. Shannon created this clever mini to capture what she felt was essential to a balanced life: "I think this container is symbolic of life," says Shannon. "You need a main dish and side dishes in the same way you need a good mix of family time, work time and play time."

Using the container as a template, Shannon created three mini books to fit in each compartment. Consider other containers you can use to store a mini book that you can take with you to remind yourself of what really matters most.

Try This!

Use this mini for documenting:

- The things you love about each person in your family
- Favorites
- Vacations

A BALANCED LIFE *by Shannon Taylor.*
Supplies *Patterned paper:* SEI, We R Memory Keepers and American Crafts; *Velvet letter stickers:* American Crafts; *Paint:* Delta Creative; *Ring fasteners:* Junkitz; *Chipboard shape:* BasicGrey; *Adhesive:* Therm O Web; *Fonts:* Ghostrider, Fontleroy Brown and Moseley, Internet; *Other:* Tupperware container and chipboard box.

Papaw Bob is quite the character. He acts like a toughy but really he's a softy of the heart. He comes from a large family of mostly girls except for his fraternal twin brother. He lives on the same land he was born on. He served in the military for a short time but worked most his life at Graybar Electric. He's a hard working man who loves to watch his grandson play baseball. He acts like he doesn't like to babysit, but never ever turns us down. He's a stinker.

My working space isn't the biggest space, but it works for me. I get teased for this but I bring my portable DVD player to work every day & listen to movies. Yes.... I listen. It totally keeps me productive. On my desk sits a scrapbook page of my 2 boys, fun little post-it notes from my friend & quite often my Lean Cuisine lunch or dinner.

BRADLEY'S CHECKUP

12

by Heidi Sonboul

DOCUMENT A POSITIVE EXPERIENCE AT THE DOCTOR OR DENTIST

The first day of school, a trip to the doctor's office or the first time with a babysitter can be a source of anxiety, so if your little one has a great experience, create a mini to celebrate it! It's an excellent way to reinforce the positive event, and it's sure to be a project your child will enjoy looking at.

Learn how to create this type of mini using just two sheets of cardstock, like Heidi did, by checking out our reference section on page 153.

Try This!

Use this mini for documenting:

- A first school performance
- A camping adventure
- The completion of a difficult school assignment

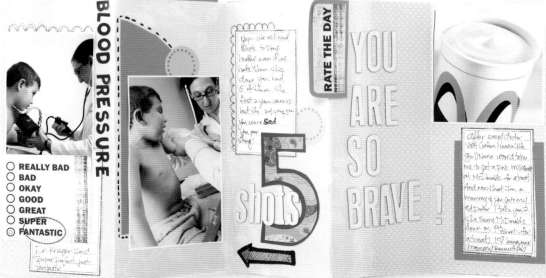

BRADLEY'S CHECKUP *by Heidi Sonboul.*

Supplies *Cardstock:* Bazzill Basics Paper; *Patterned paper:* Heidi Grace Designs, My Mind's Eye, Hot Off The Press, Making Memories, Heidi Swapp for Advantus and Autumn Leaves; *Letter stickers:* Deflect-o; *Chipboard letters and numbers:* Heidi Swapp for Advantus; *Brad:* Making Memories; *Acrylic arrows:* Hot Off The Press; *Labels:* My Mind's Eye; *Button:* Autumn Leaves; *Pen:* American Crafts; *Font:* Times New Roman, Microsoft.

chapter 2

Memorabilia

A MINI IS A GREAT PLACE TO STORE MEMORABILIA—movie tickets, receipts, brochures, e-mails, handwritten notes, things kids bring home from school, clothing tags, maps and the stuff of life that accumulates on the counter . . . and on the dresser . . . and on the desk. *We all have it.* Give it a home in a mini book. And if the item is too big to fit in a mini without altering it, feel free to do as some of the designers have done here and go with a larger album size. What's important is organizing these real, true pieces of life so you can enjoy them in the future.

I have a small vintage suitcase in my office just to hold these cool little bits of life. When you create your next project, enhance your story with something you've gathered from your own personal experiences.

A NOTE ABOUT ARCHIVAL SAFETY: *If you're concerned about the archival quality of any of the items you're scrapbooking (newspaper clippings, receipts, business cards), treat them with a deacidification spray before adding them to your album. If it's not important to you to use originals, consider scanning, printing and scrapbooking copies instead.*

Use this mini for documenting:

- Important school papers or good grades
- Certificates of achievement
- Extracurricular awards or newspaper clippings

MAINTAIN AN ORGANIZED FILE OF IMPORTANT SCHOOL RECORDS

From academics to sports, Laura's husband has a ton of memorabilia from his college career at the Naval Academy. Laura wanted to create a special, organized place to maintain these records at their original sizes, even if they were too large to feature in a traditional mini. As a solution, she divided all the memorabilia and photos into sections—Admissions, Plebe Summer, Plebe Year, etc.—and organized an 8½" x 11" album into those categories.

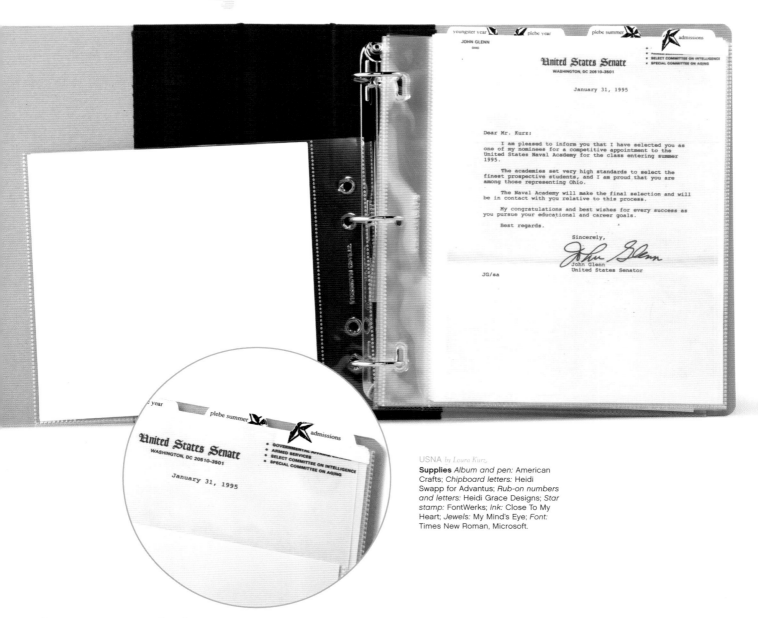

USNA *by Laura Kurz*

Supplies *Album and pen:* American Crafts; *Chipboard letters:* Heidi Swapp for Advantus; *Rub-on numbers and letters:* Heidi Grace Designs; *Star stamp:* FontWerks; *Ink:* Close To My Heart; *Jewels:* My Mind's Eye; *Font:* Times New Roman, Microsoft.

KEEP A RECORD OF THE ORDINARY, EVERYDAY MEMORABILIA

If you love to go antiquing, you know the thrill of finding the everyday artifacts and mementos from an earlier time—old postcards, photos, etc. So why not preserve a piece of the present for the future?

Emily created this handy 6" x 8" mini by taking all the stuff from her daily life that she might ordinarily throw away—receipts, candy wrappers, kids' doodles, tickets, business cards—and sewing them down on a base page (to save time, you can decoupage them on cardstock or chipboard instead). Says Emily, "Years from now, I know it's going to be so much fun to look back over the little things that were part of our daily lives. I want to save a little part of each month for a year—proof of our lives for future generations to enjoy."

PROOF OF LIFE *by Emily Falconbridge.*
Supplies *Patterned paper:* Autumn Leaves and BasicGrey; *Rub-ons:* BasicGrey, 7gypsies and Creative Imaginations; *Letter stickers:* Making Memories; *Stamp and month cards:* 7gypsies; *Gel medium:* Matisse Derivan; *Digital label:* Swank Label by Jennifer Pebbles, *www.twopeasinabucket.com;* *Other:* Vintage ledger paper, binder rings and chipboard.

Use this mini for
documenting:

- Christmas cards
- Birthday cards
- A high school
  senior's collection of
  graduation notices
  and invitations

KEEP IMPORTANT FAMILY
ANNOUNCEMENTS IN ONE PLACE

Maggie wanted an easy way to store all the wedding and birth
announcements she receives from family and friends. "I've always
wanted to save them, but I've never had a great place to keep them
together," she explains. A mini was the perfect solution! Maggie created a larger album (12" x 9") to accommodate the various card sizes.

For the book spine, Maggie cut a 9" x 3½" piece of heavy cardstock.
She used one interoffice-type envelope with a string-and-button
closure for her front and back covers. She cut the portion with the
button closure as the front cover and used the back half of the envelope (including the envelope flap) as the back cover, stitching both
to the spine. For the inner pages, she gathered a variety of different
envelopes, folding the bottom ¼" of each and stitching them to the
spine, then layering each envelope on top of the previous until the
entire spine was filled. To finish, she tucked cards, photos, and wedding and birth announcements inside the envelope "pages." You can
also sew in the actual envelopes you receive to create your pages.

REMEMBER *by Maggie Holmes.*
Supplies *Patterned paper:* Making Memories; *Letter stickers:* American Crafts and Scrapworks; *Rub-ons:* Art
Warehouse, Creative Imaginations; *Transparency:* My Mind's Eye; *Envelopes:* Bazzill Basics Paper and unknown;
Other: Buttons.

CREATE A PERSONAL DIRECTORY
OF FAVORITE LOCAL SPOTS

Wouldn't you love to know where your great-grandparents shopped
or spent time when they were your age? Better yet, wouldn't you
like to share the places you love with visiting friends who have similar tastes? Maria Grace created this 4" x 4" personal directory/
address book to introduce visitors to her favorite places.
"I added the blank library cards so I could add quick notes or
reminders to myself about upcoming visits to these spots." She
attached a strip of elastic to the right-hand pages so she could insert
business cards as she collects them. For the binding, she used a
beaded chain so she can easily add extra pages or categories. (*Note:*
For a sturdier binding, you can also use jumbo binder rings.)

Did You Notice?

Maria Grace adhered strips of ribbon to the right-hand pages and slipped business cards beneath them. You can also use strips of elastic or fabric.

To ensure that cards will be held in place securely, apply adhesive above and below the areas you intend to hold the cards.

PERSONAL 411 *by Maria Grace Abuzman.*

Supplies *Patterned paper:* FontWerks, Fancy Pants Designs, Hambly Studios, Sassafras Lass and KI Memories; *Stamps:* FontWerks, Provo Craft and Stampin' Up!; *Ink:* Ranger Industries; *Stickers:* American Crafts, FontWerks, Heidi Grace Designs, Jenni Bowlin Studio and Heidi Swapp for Advantus; *Corner punch:* Fiskars; *Chipboard pages:* Bazzill Basics Paper; *Other:* Beaded chain, large eyelets and library cards; *Other:* Ribbon.

SO THIS IS WHAT FIVE LOOKS LIKE
17
by Mou Saha

Time flies when children are growing, and before you know it, you've forgotten many of the little details you thought you'd remember forever. Mou didn't want that to happen, so she decided to save some of her daughter's memorabilia and photos in an 8" x 6" book made out of file folders and envelopes—it fits perfectly within a 9" x 7½" wooden box, along with some oversized and dimensional memorabilia.

She had her daughter write in her answers to a questionnaire and preserved her handprint to capture this fun and unique glimpse of her life at the age of five.

Note: For original, one-of-a-kind memorabilia, make copies or treat the originals with a deacidification spray. Also, if you're storing items in a wood box, be aware that wood naturally contains acid, so it's a good idea to treat the box with the spray, as well as apply a few coats of decoupage medium after painting or decorating.

Try This!

Use this mini for documenting:

- A pet at a certain age
- Baby's memorabilia
- All the paperwork and photos associated with a loved one's favorite car, sport, etc.

SO THIS IS WHAT FIVE LOOKS LIKE *by Mou Saha.*
Supplies *Wood box:* Don Mechanic Enterprises, Ltd.; *Patterned paper:* Frances Meyer; *Die cuts:* Autumn Leaves (tags) and K&Company (labels); *Metal and chipboard photo corners:* Making Memories; *Rub-on letters:* American Crafts; *Stickers:* Die Cuts With a View (epoxy) and Heidi Swapp for Advantus (red letters and number); *Paint:* Delta Creative; *Stamps:* Autumn Leaves and K&Company; *Ink:* Tsukineko; *Gaffer tape:* 7gypsies; *Chipboard "5":* Prima; *Clear tabs:* Wal-Mart; *Embroidery floss:* DMC; *Glaze:* Mod Podge, Plaid Enterprises.

FAVORITES @ 5

color — Pink
song — ABCD
book — Home sweet home
food — Grapes
person — Mom
when i grow up i want to be — Artist and ballerina

September 1, 2007

I like to Pa+o

September 24, 2007

I love my mom and dad and baby.

FRIENDS

An Invitation

Matters of heart

WHEN YOU LOOK AT ME, WHEN YOU THINK OF ME, I AM IN PARADISE.

WILLIAM MAKEPEACE THACKERAY

chapter 3

Collections

WHAT DO YOU OR YOUR FAMILY MEMBERS COLLECT? Maybe it's trains, artwork, cars or tea cups. Whatever it is, those pieces are stories waiting to be told. A person's collections often reveal an intimate view of a life, a passion. Collectors tend to have very specific stories related to the what, why, where and when of their collections.

As you begin to think about documenting your story or that of someone you love, try to answer these questions: Why do you collect what you do? When did you begin? Will you ever have enough? How do you store your collection? What would you like family and friends to know about your collection in the years to come? Will this collection be passed on?

old is new

Try This!

Use this mini for documenting:

- A typical shopping list for your family
- Favorite before-school purchases
- Gifts family members received at Christmas

CREATE A HANDY SHOPPING GUIDE OR LIST FOR ANTIQUING

For the last few years, I've been acquiring a variety of things (from furniture and fabric to organizational pieces and art) from second-hand, junk and antique stores. So I designed this 4" x 6" book to help me remember and document my collection of antique and second-hand finds. The small size makes this perfect for throwing in my bag whenever I'm out and about. Now I have a record of my finds and a place to make notes about things I'm looking for as well as measurements from my home, prices, colors, etc. The pocket pages are a great place to keep receipts and additional documentation.

OLD IS NEW *by Ali Edwards.*
Supplies *Album:* Sarabinders, Hot Off The Press; *Patterned paper:* Danny O for K&Company; *Fabric stickers:* 7gypsies; *Crackle paint:* Tim Holtz Distress Crackle Paint, Ranger Industries; *Rub-ons:* 7gypsies and Jenni Bowlin Studio; *Fonts:* SchoolHouse and 1942 Report, Internet; *Other:* Library cards.

AUTHOR *looking* FOR:

TITLE

DATE DUE   BORROWER'S NAME

Π typewriter
"tall light"

old is new

SEARCH

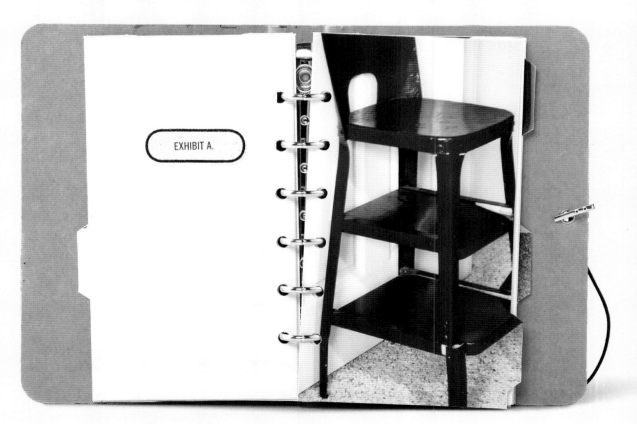

EXHIBIT A.

CLICK CLICK CLICK

19 *by Ali Edwards*

This is a 7½" x 4¾" book for my son, Simon, that features a collection of photos he's taken over the last couple of years in the different homes we've lived in. I love these premade albums with 4" x 6" page protectors because they're easy—just slip in your photos and go. Not every photo needs a long story to go along with it; not every photo needs to be on a scrapbook page either—sometimes they work just as well in a nice little book like this. You can always create a 4" x 6" journaling block and slip it into one of the sleeves.

As an introduction to this album on the inside front cover, I created a little spot for journaling with patterned paper and a photo. To finish it off, I used a rub-on along the bottom that unifies the elements, stuck on letters for Simon's initials and used one set of arrow stamps. The inside pages are all photos.

Try This!

Use this mini for documenting:

- A collection of school photos from kindergarten through high school
- Your child's favorite artwork (for example, all of his pictures of his family through the years)
- Handwriting samples as it changes through the years

CLICK, CLICK, CLICK *by Ali Edwards.*

Supplies *Album:* SEI; *Patterned paper:* Jenni Bowlin Studio, Pebbles Inc. and K&Company; *Word stickers:* 7gypsies; *Foam letter stickers and pen:* American Crafts; *Star stickers:* Cavallini & Co.; *Rub-on line:* Jenni Bowlin Studio.

THE STORY OF YOUR TOYS

20

by Ali Edwards

What child doesn't hold particular toys and objects dear? As the years pass, don't you wish you could look back on those items that once brought you so much comfort and happiness? And most of us have some sort of "toys" as adults. What are your toys right now?

As a kid, I had a ton of favorite toys. Some were around for just a bit, and some were around for much longer. I wish I had a photographic record of them and how they corresponded to the different times in my life (and I wish I'd started this mini book when my son was a baby!).

One of the coolest things about mini books is that they make great homes for documenting collections or things that change over time. This 8¾" x 6" book would also be great for documenting your toys, your books, your trips—anything you want to organize—because the tabs make organization super easy.

Try This!

Use this mini for documenting:

- A loved one's favorite knickknacks
- Favorite family recipes or meals
- Family heirloom jewelry

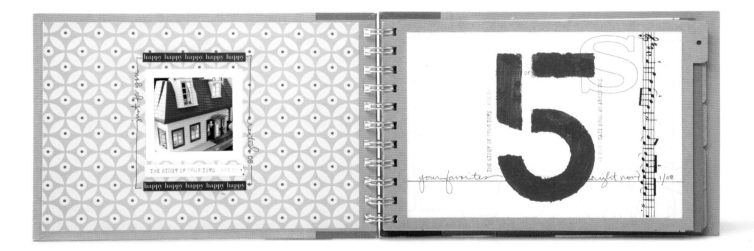

THE STORY OF YOUR TOYS *by Ali Edwards*

Supplies *Album:* Creative Café; *Cardstock:* Bazzill Basics Paper; *Patterned paper:* Cross-My-Heart; *Rub-ons:* Jenni Bowlin Studio; *Chipboard:* June Kit of the Month, Lisa Bearnson.com; *Paint:* Ranger Industries; *Transparency:* Hambly Studios; *Pen:* American Crafts; *Fonts:* Chalet, Forge and Baskerville, Internet; *Other:* Stencil.

YOUR STUFF

21

by Emily Falconbridge

PHOTOGRAPH AND RECORD
EVERYTHING A LOVED ONE COLLECTS

Some collections just can't fit in a book, things like rocks, sea shells or model cars. But the memory of these collections and how they define the people we love are still precious and worth recording. So why not take a photo of these collections and create a mini to celebrate all this special stuff?

Emily's daughter, Ivy, loves to collect all kinds of things. Says Emily, "I often find piles of dirty rocks, sticks and old fruit pits adorning the furniture in her room! I know one day she'll outgrow this stage, so I wanted to capture her 'treasures' on camera."

Emily decided to create a 4½" x 4½" album by placing her photos and journaling between two transparency sheets and sewing around the page edges. The small size makes this book a perfect treasure that Ivy can look at again and again and again!

Try This!

Use this mini for documenting:

- Travel knickknacks, like postcards
- Coins and foreign currency
- Sports memorabilia, such as baseball cards, banners and more

YOUR STUFF *by Emily Falconbridge.*

Supplies *Patterned paper:* Rouge de Garance, Jenni Bowlin Studio, Autumn Leaves, BasicGrey and My Mind's Eye; *Stickers:* 7gypsies, Making Memories and Heidi Swapp for Advantus; *Rub-ons:* American Crafts, BasicGrey and Creative Imaginations; *Other:* Transparency sheets and masking tape.

A FOND
COLLECTION

22 *by Mou Saha*

Mou created this 9" x 9" album for her father, an art lover who has been collecting this particular artist's work for two decades. While the album celebrates this wonderful collection of art memorabilia, Mou actually created it as a thank-you to her father, sharing her gratitude for the inspiration the artist has given her.

Mou selected a premade album that came with a window for the title on the cover and an elastic band for closure. Drawing inspiration from the artist, Mou painted a figurine around the title window, with the cloth cover serving as her canvas. To include the art catalogs in this mini, she created jumbo photo corners by simply folding black cardstock into triangles and adhering them to the pages.

Try This!

Use this mini for documenting:

- Correspondence with a distant friend or pen pal
- Love letters
- Concert booklets and flyers

A FOND COLLECTION *by Mou Saha.*

Supplies *Album:* Heidi Swapp for Advantus; *Cardstock:* Frances Meyer (black) and The Paper Company (mango and cream); *Label die cut (used as template):* Autumn Leaves; *Stamps:* FontWerks (letters, frame and brackets), 7gypsies (rectangle label) and Martha Stewart Crafts (swirly label); *Ink:* Ranger Industries; *Colored crayon:* Magic Fx Crazy Chromatic Coloring Pencil, Koh-I-Noor, Chartpak; *Embroidery floss:* DMC; *Scallop-edge scissors:* Provo Craft; *Paint:* Delta Creative; *Pen:* Marvy Uchida; *Font:* Arial, www.dafont.com.

chapter 4

Gift Albums

ONE OF THE MOST BEAUTIFUL ASPECTS OF SCRAPBOOKING is creating books to give away. Mini books are perfect for gifts simply because of their size and the ability to produce multiples in much less time than it takes to create a large 12" x 12" album.

When creating gifts for others, I tend to go with a very simple approach. Recipients will enjoy the handmade touch, and whether you add photos and journaling or leave the pages blank for them to fill in, you're sharing a special gift from the heart that they'll treasure.

Use this gift mini for:

- Pet photos
- Fun photo strips from photo booths
- Photos of your circle of friends

SHOW OFF THE LATEST FAMILY PICTURES IN A FUN BRAG BOOK

A stylish photo mini is a great gift for grandparents or teachers. They can tuck it in a bag to show off while waiting in line at the airport, or they can simply display it on a shelf at home.

Maggie created this 4¾" x 6" grandparents' brag book by covering a slide-mount holder with paper and paint, embellishing with rub-ons and stickers, and cutting her photos to fit inside the slide-mount spaces. "The slide-mount holder was perfect because we have four kids and it had four spaces," says Maggie. "The spaces also work well for showing multiple photos of one child or for journaling."

HUGS AND KISSES *by Maggie Holmes.*
Supplies *Patterned paper:* Hambly Studios, Scenic Route and Making Memories; *Chipboard sticker, letter stickers, paint and tape:* Making Memories; *Pen:* Zig Millennium, EK Success; *Other:* Slide-mount holder.

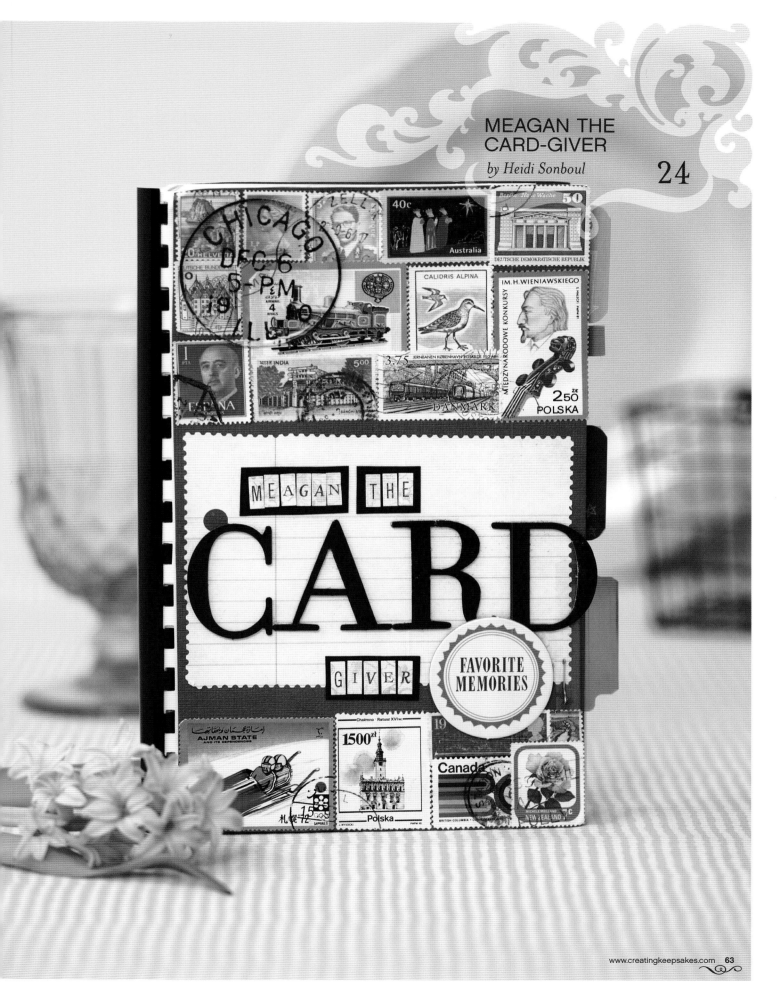

Use this gift mini for:

- Special-event and sporting-event tickets
- School programs
- Postcards from travels

CREATE A CLEVER BOOK OF GREETING CARDS RECEIVED BY LOVED ONES

Wondering what to do with all those cards you receive for birthdays or special occasions? Rather than storing them in a memorabilia box or a desk drawer, put a new spin on them by turning them into a mini book. A mini like this makes a perfect anniversary gift filled with years of love letters. It's also a fabulous way to celebrate a friendship, like Heidi did here, by showcasing all the cards, letters and postcards you've exchanged through the years.

To create this 8½" x 5" book, Heidi used a bookbinding machine to punch holes in each card. Then, she opened up the plastic spiral binding and carefully layered each card so they're all visible.

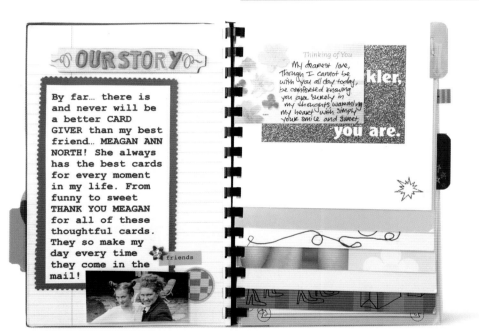

MEAGAN THE CARD-GIVER
by Heidi Sonboul.
Supplies *Cardstock:* Bazzill Basics Paper; *Patterned paper:* Making Memories and Heidi Swapp for Advantus; *Page tabs:* Target, K&Company and Scenic Route.

You're such a good friend that if I had a new biker boyfriend, you wouldn't roll your eyes every time I said.

Don't you start, because then I'll start and you'll make that face and I'll make that snorting noise and then we'll both be in trouble and I didn't even start it!

Hallmark
F R E S H | I N K

www.hallmark.com

U.S.A. 2.29
Canada 3.29
YYF 250-2
© HALLMARK LICENSING, INC.
HALLMARK CARDS, INC.
KANSAS CITY, MO 64141
TORONTO, CANADA M2J 1P6
MADE IN U.S.A.
RES. PHOTO

day every time they come in the mail!

friends

Walt Disney's
Cinderella

Shoebox
(A tiny little division of Hallmark)

www.hallmark.com
www.shoebox.com

PRODUCT MADE OF RECYCLED PAPER:
minimum 20% post-consumer fiber

U.S.A. 2.49
Canada 3.49
ZF 59-4
HALLMARK CARDS, INC.
KANSAS CITY, MO 64141
TORONTO, CANADA M2J 1P6
MADE IN U.S.A.

TO PROVE MY FRIENDSHIP FOR YOU, I WOULD EAT AN ENTIRE CHEESECAKE BY MYSELF IN ONE SITTING.

THIS IS YOU

25

by Maria Grace Abuzman

CREATE A FUNKY FILL-IN-THE-BLANK
SCRAPBOOK FOR A FRIEND

Introduce a friend to scrapbooking by creating a beautiful fill-in mini, complete with journaling prompts. Maria Grace designed this 3¼" x 8" scrapbook using a chipboard-album base; she simply added decorative wrapping paper to the cover and used patterned paper to decorate the interior pages. To create a place to tuck in the interactive journaling tags, she applied double-sided adhesive along the bottom of glassine envelopes and attached them to her pages. Then, she created the fill-in tags with ribbon, cardstock, tabs and decorative stamps.

Says Maria Grace, "I wanted to give my friend a book where she can add photos and write her thoughts down as well. This size allows her to crop or use smaller photos of herself."

Try This!

Use this gift mini for:
- Tweens and teens
- Notes and memorabilia about favorite books
- Movie and concert tickets

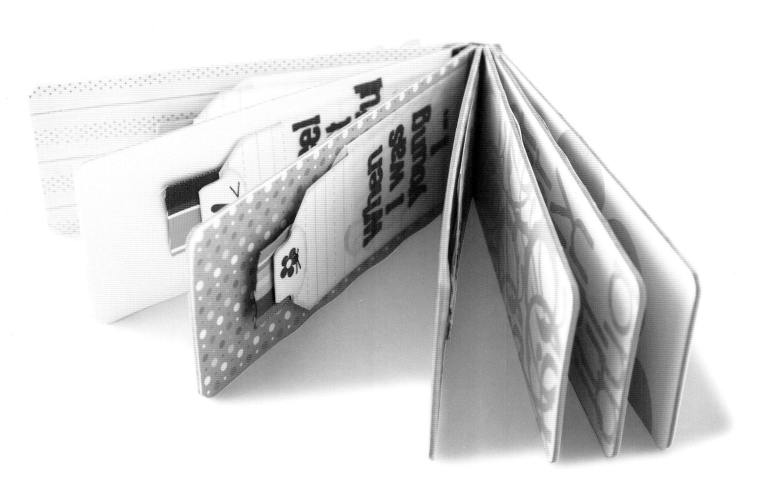

THIS IS YOU *by Maria Grace Abuzman.*

Supplies *Software:* Adobe Illustrator, Adobe Systems; *Album:* Cloud 9 Design, Fiskars; *Cardstock:* Martha Stewart Crafts and Paper Source; *Patterned paper:* Fancy Pants Designs, Hambly Studios, Heidi Grace Designs, KI Memories and Making Memories; *Wrapping paper and glassine envelopes:* Paper Source; *Ribbon:* Heidi Grace Designs and Strano Designs; *Stamps:* Doodlebug Design, FontWerks and Lakeshore; *Ink:* Ranger Industries; *Foam stamps:* Kit of the Month, Creating Keepsakes; *Paint:* Blick; *Glitter:* Martha Stewart Crafts; *Notch tool and corner rounder:* Fiskars; *Button:* Autumn Leaves; *Die-cut machine:* QuicKutz; *Font:* Clarendon, Internet; *Other:* Staples.

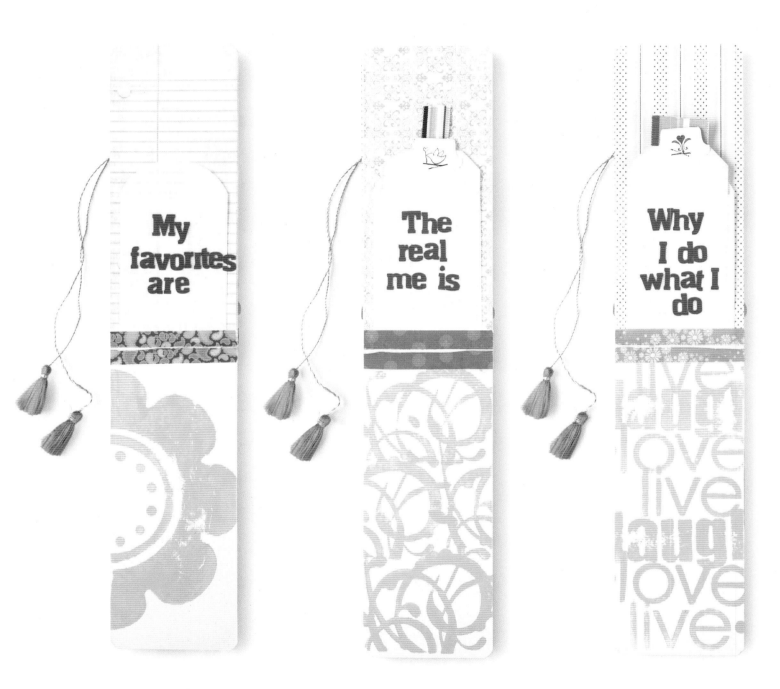

Try This!

Use this gift mini for:

- A school notebook for a tween or teen
- A diary for a young girl
- An artist's notebook

SHARE YOUR CREATIVE FLAIR
WITH A DECORATIVE BLANK JOURNAL

Blank notebooks and journals are perfect gifts for anyone on your list. "I love them—there's so much possibility for creativity on each page!" says Emily, who created this gorgeous 6" x 9" blank journal using leftover scraps of cardstock, patterned paper, envelopes and tags. She attached the bits together to form pages with a sewing machine.

Score each piece to form a spine, then layer your pages on top of each other as you go. Once you have a big enough stack, line up the spines on each page and carefully sew them together using a denim needle in your sewing machine. You can also use staples, tape or hand-stitching to form your pages. For her creative cover, Emily placed the finished mini within a knit wrap with a simple button closure. (Two strips of yarn wrap around a button "notch.")

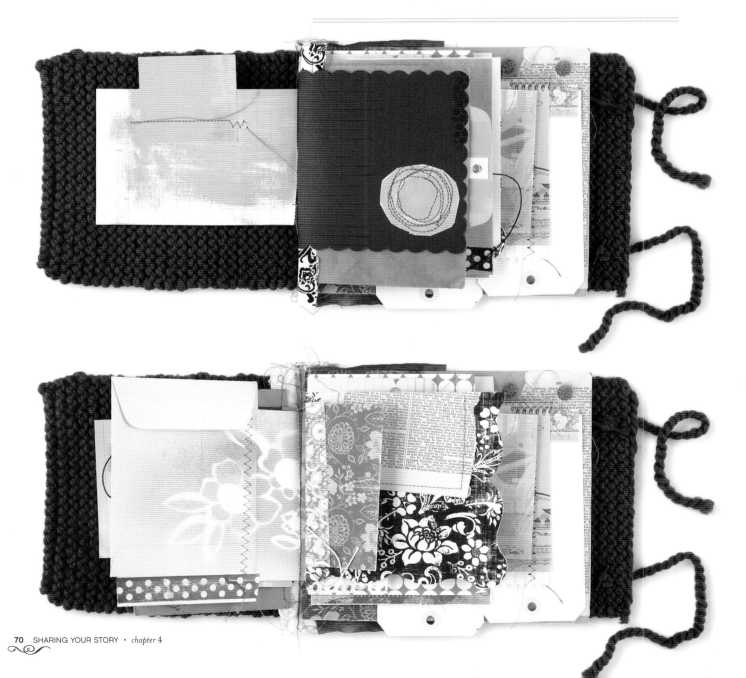

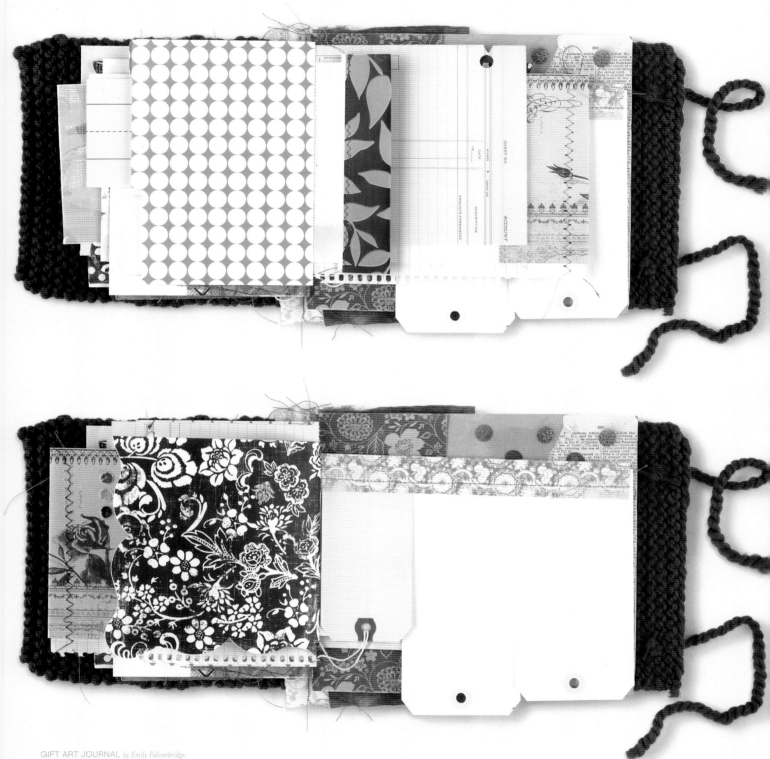

GIFT ART JOURNAL *by Emily Falconbridge.*
Supplies *Cardstock:* Bazzill Basics Paper; *Patterned papers:* Autumn Leaves, BasicGrey, My Mind's Eye and Making Memories; *Rub-ons and die cuts:* BasicGrey; *Tape, file folders and masks:* Heidi Swapp for Advantus; *Stickers:* 7gypsies; *Buttons:* Autumn Leaves; *Other:* Vintage book text, tags, fabric, handmade paper, yarn, spray paint, envelopes and ephemera.

A GIFT FOR YOU, PRINCESS ANUSHA

27 *by Mou Saha*

MAKE A FUN FILL-IN ALBUM FOR A CHILD

Mou created this special 6" x 6" album as a gift for her five-year-old daughter, who is a big fan of the Disney princess characters. "I wanted to give her an album where she could collect autographs of her favorite princesses on one of our frequent visits to the park," she says.

Inspired by thoughts of glass slippers, flowers and jewels, Mou opted for a flower-shaped clear acrylic album, held together by a binder ring. She added a 26" ribbon through the ring and fastened on a bead to keep the ribbon in place.

Try This!

Use this gift mini for:

· End-of the-school-year notes
· Reflections on a child's birthday each year
· Teen friendship book

A GIFT FOR YOU,
PRINCESS ANUSHA
by Mou Saha.
Supplies *Flower-shaped album:* Rusty Pickle; *Patterned paper:* Frances Meyer (dot) and Die Cuts With a View (pink); *Gems:* me & my BIG ideas; *Rub-ons:* Die Cuts With a View; *Gift tag:* FontWerks; *Acrylic heart:* Heidi Swapp for Advantus; *Disney-themed bottle caps:* EK Success; *Fabric flowers:* Autumn Leaves; *Stamps:* 7gypsies; *Ink:* Tsukineko; *Ribbon and beads:* Michaels; *Other:* Rubber mallet and paper towels.

chapter 5

Collaborative Books

MINIS ARE THE PERFECT FORMAT FOR BOOKS CREATED BY MORE THAN ONE PERSON. Collaborative books offer viewers an opportunity to add their own thoughts, photos, accents and more, whether it's a guest book for your home (welcoming visitors and documenting their stay), a wedding book or a memorial book for a loved one who's passed away.

Collaborative albums can also be shared between friends or relatives across the miles. Create a book that you send back and forth. Embellish a page, tell a story and add accents, then send it to a friend or family member. What a cool way to document the passage of time, reflect on the time we live in and celebrate a friendship.

Use this mini for documenting:

- Friends attending a bridal shower
- Book club meetings
- Holiday parties or gatherings you attend

CREATE A VISUAL RECORD OF GUESTS WHO VISIT YOUR HOME

One of my favorite things to do whenever we rent a house in the mountains or at the beach is to leaf through the guest book. I love to read about others' experiences—what they enjoyed, why they were there. This inspired me to create the same type of book for my own home to document the guests who visit from time to time.

To create my 7½" x 5" guest book, I decorated the album's chipboard cover with fabric and a vintage decorative accent, and adhered patterned paper to the inside of the cover. Then I punched holes for the binder rings. I covered the interior pages with patterned paper, sticking to a neutral black/gray/beige color scheme. On each album spread, I added patterned paper, room for a bit of journaling from me or our guests, a photo and a swatch of a transparency with the family's initial. I used photo corners to keep the photos in place.

GUEST BOOK by Ali Edwards.
Supplies Album: 7gypsies; Patterned paper: Anna Griffin and Scenic Route; Fabric: Cocoa Daisy November 2007 Kit; Cover charm: Jenni Bowlin Studio; Transparency: Hambly Studios; Letter accents: Narratives, Creative Imaginations; Rub-ons: 7gypsies; Font: Chalet, Internet; Other: Photo corners.

Try This!

Use this mini for documenting:

- Your relationship with a close friend or neighbor who is moving away
- A pet's life
- Favorite gifts given to or received by a favorite relative or friend

SHARE HOW SOMEONE HAS TOUCHED YOUR LIFE

Create a meaningful and heartfelt memorial album by designing a format that friends and family can easily add to. Amanda created this 4" x 6" album to honor her father at his funeral. "We put out stacks of 3" x 5" note cards and asked people to jot down favorite memories," she says. "I appreciated that so many people took the time to fill out these cards for us, creating something special that my siblings, my mom and I will treasure."

If you think loved ones might be intimidated by the thought of having to write directly in an album, providing note cards that you adhere later is a terrific way to encourage everyone to participate. After compiling everyone's journaling cards, Amanda rounded the corners and inked the edges, paired them with coordinating photos and adhered them in this little album.

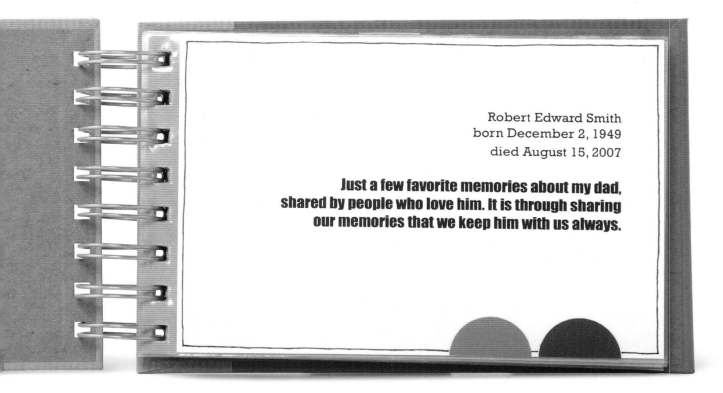

Robert Edward Smith
born December 2, 1949
died August 15, 2007

Just a few favorite memories about my dad, shared by people who love him. It is through sharing our memories that we keep him with us always.

SHARE *by Amanda Probst.*

Supplies *Software:* Adobe Photoshop CS2, Adobe Systems; *Cardstock:* Prism Papers; *Patterned paper:* Making Memories; *Corner rounder and circle punch:* EK Success; *Ink:* ColorBox, Clearsnap; *Pen:* Precision Pen, American Crafts; *Font:* Impact, Microsoft.

One of the many great memories of Robert is him riding off in the convertible Volkswagon after he & Mary had their marriage renewal vows at the church. He had such a sweet smile and was so joyous with Mary at his side! I love Robert and will miss him so very much. He had the "gift."

Love, Lillian

God
doesn't look at
how much we do,
but with
how much love
we do it.

MOTHER TERESA

June 2002

One of my favorite memories of Robert was when he full on tackled me playing two vs two football over thanksgiving of 2006. Super-man just came out of nowhere and took me out! It was amazing! I love you Robert

always,
Ana

Nov 1994

SENIOR YEAR

30 *by Laura Kurz*

PREPARE FOR A MEMORABLE SCHOOL
YEAR WITH A STYLISH FILL-IN ALBUM

Laura created this cool 9" x 6" mini for her cousin to fill out each month during her senior year in high school. "My cousin, Devin, loves to take photos, but she hasn't started scrapbooking," Laura explains. "I wanted to get her started or at least give her a place to write and keep her memories of her senior year."

Laura designed the album so each month is similar, with a spot for journaling, a spot for photos and a modified folder for memorabilia.

Try This!

Use this mini for documenting:

- Sports activities for the year
- First-time experiences or school performances
- School achievements, such as honor roll or science fair

SENIOR YEAR *by Laura Kurz.*
Supplies *Album:* Making Memories; *Patterned paper:* Anna Griffin; *Month stamp:* Kit of the Month, *Creating Keepsakes; Rub-on letters:* Heidi Grace Designs; *Flash cards:* 7gypsies; *Paint:* Making Memories; *Butterfly mask:* Heidi Swapp for Advantus; *Pen:* American Crafts.

celebrate
&remember

REMEMBER A LOVED ONE WITH A CLASSIC GIFT ALBUM

If you prefer a more formal and traditional feel for your collaborative mini album, choose a neutral color scheme and add features like vellum overlays, as Maria Grace did for this memorial album she designed as a gift. "I inserted vellum between each page to mimic the style of older scrapbooks," she says. Each vellum sheet features a label sticker and a stamped frame image, while each album page provides room for a photo and displays a quote.

When creating a memorial album as a gift, Maria Grace advises designing the album so the recipient and her family can easily fill it out and finish it with their own photos.

Try This!

Use this mini for documenting:

- Family histories
- A wedding
- Old family or baby photos

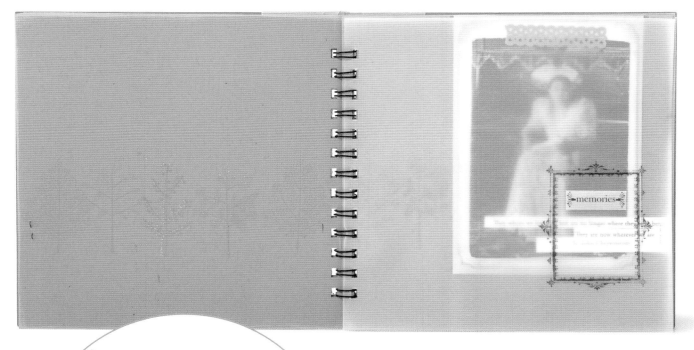

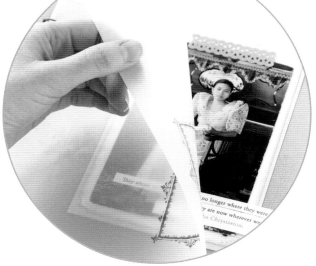

CELEBRATE & REMEMBER
by Maria Grace Abuzman.
Supplies *Software:* Adobe InDesign, Adobe Systems; *Cardstock:* Martha Stewart Crafts and Paper Source; *Vellum and fabric cover:* Paper Source; *Stickers:* Heidi Grace Designs, Li'l Davis Designs, Making Memories and Heidi Swapp for Advantus; *Stamps:* FontWerks and Hero Arts; *Ink:* Ranger Industries and Tsukineko; *Rub-ons:* Heidi Grace Designs; *Decorative corner punch:* Fiskars; *Paper trim:* Creative Imaginations; *Clear embossing powder:* Ranger Industries; *Binding:* Zutter Innovative Products; *Font:* Garamond, Microsoft; *Other:* Staples.

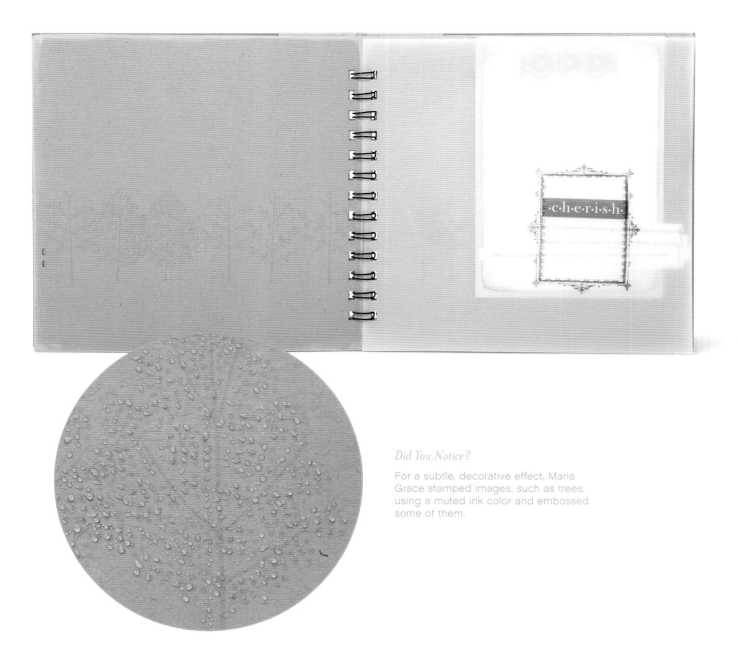

Did You Notice?

For a subtle, decorative effect, Maria Grace stamped images, such as trees, using a muted ink color and embossed some of them.

Try This!

Use this mini for
documenting:

· A coworker's birthday

· A teacher's gift

· A welcome to a
  new family in the
  neighborhood

DESIGN A MINI BOOK FILLED
WITH BIRTHDAY WISHES AND NOTES

A collaborative mini book makes a wonderful gift for a loved one.
Show him how special he is by including comments and well-wishes
from everyone in the family.

Maggie created this 8" x 6" mini for her son's birthday. To begin,
she cut her cardstock cover and interior patterned pages to size.
Then she folded all the pages in half and stitched down the center
to create the binding. (You can also staple or hand-stitch along the
center to bind the pages.) After embellishing the book, Maggie
asked family members to write a personal message to her son and
then presented the completed book to him on his birthday.

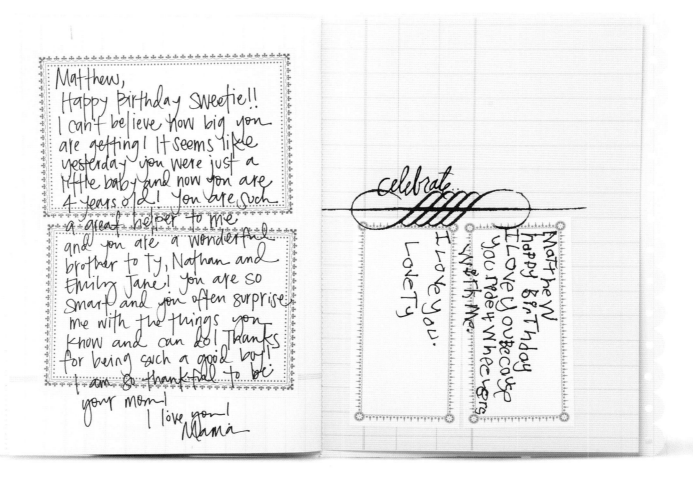

HAPPY BIRTHDAY, MATTHEW *by Maggie Holmes.*

Supplies *Patterned paper:* Creative Imaginations and Making Memories; *Rub-ons:* Making Memories and
American Crafts; *Chipboard letters:* Heidi Swapp for Advantus; *Chipboard glitter stars:* Making Memories;
Pen: Zig Millennium, EK Success; *Other:* Notebook paper and labels.

Try This!

Use this mini for documenting:

· The friends your child meets at summer camp

· Guests to your home

· Family holiday activites

MAKE AN ARTFUL JOURNAL AT A BABY SHOWER

Shower books are a great way to involve all the attendees at a party or shower while creating a memorable keepsake for the honoree! Maria Grace created this 5" x 7" shower book with versatility in mind. "I used binder rings so the pages would be easy to remove and distribute to the guests attending the shower," she explains. For the interior pages, she started with a 5" x 7" piece of cardstock for her last page and then trimmed 1" from each subsequent sheet in the album for a staggered effect. For another fun touch, she used a different border punch along the bottom of each sheet.

Maria Grace created several different sizes of journaling spots on each page so guests could choose to write just a little or a lot, depending on their personal preference. For added flexibility, consider providing additional scrapbook papers and accents at the event so guests can further embellish the pages or journaling blocks if they'd like.

HEY, BABY *by Maria Grace Abuzman.*
Supplies *Cardstock:* Paper Source and Martha Stewart Crafts; *Patterned paper:* Heidi Grace Designs, KI Memories, My Mind's Eye, Creative Imaginations and Paper Source; *Die-cut paper:* KI Memories; *Clear overlay:* Hambly Studios; *Border punches:* Fiskars; *Stickers:* 7gypsies, Autumn Leaves, Chronicle Books, FontWerks, Heidi Grace Designs, Heidi Swapp for Advantus, Making Memories and Creative Imaginations; *Stamps:* Bam Pop, FontWerks, Hero Arts, Provo Craft and Creating Keepsakes; *Ink:* Ranger Industries; *Rub-ons:* Autumn Leaves, BasicGrey, Hambly Studios, Heidi Grace Designs and Jenni Bowlin Studio; *Chipboard accents:* Jenni Bowlin Studio, KI Memories and Heidi Swapp for Advantus; *Transparencies:* Heidi Swapp for Advantus and Making Memories; *Metal label frame:* BasicGrey; *Other:* Binder rings and eyelets.

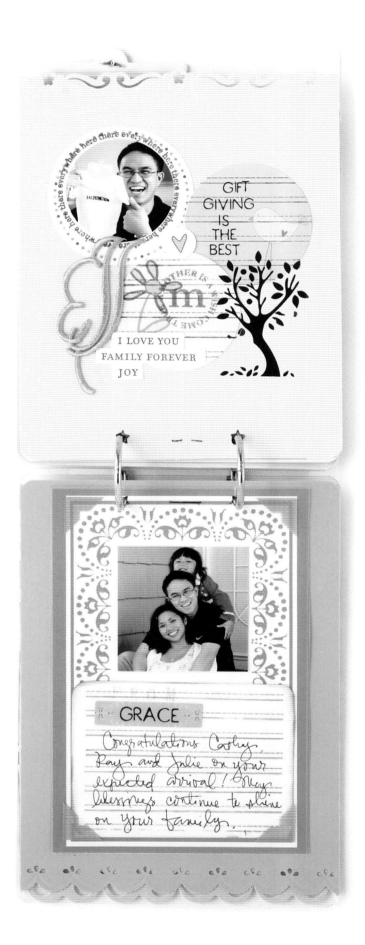

chapter 6

Books for Kids

LET'S FACE IT, MOST KIDS LOVE BOOKS, so why not create minis as educational tools? Minis can be great educational tools. They can teach numbers, colors and letters—and they can teach kids about your family's stories. In our home, mini books have become a go-to tool for preparing Simon for new experiences. We create social stories that let him know what will happen when and where, and what he can expect.

Most kids also simply love looking at photos of their family members. They are so *good* at celebrating life. Whether they document your son's soccer team or your daughter's love of art, minis are perfect for preserving family stories and experiences in a format your kids will love thumbing through again and again.

CREATE A BOOK TO TEACH A CHILD TO COUNT

Try This!

Use this mini for teaching:

- Basic numbers and counting
- Foreign-language phrases
- The alphabet

One of my favorite things about my scrapbook supplies is that I can use them for a variety of purposes. In looking through my supplies, I noticed I have a lot of numbers and alphabets—perfect for teaching Simon basic math, something he's working on in school right now. This 8½" x 4" book can travel with us for on-the-go learning.

COUNTING *by Ali Edwards.*
Supplies *Album:* Top Line Creations; *Patterned paper:* Creative Café and KI Memories; *Letter stickers:* Reminisce; *Rub-ons:* 7gypsies and American Crafts; *Stamps:* Stampers Anonymous, Savvy Stamps, Make An Impression, Rachel Greig for Stamp-It, Rebekka Erickson for Stamp World, and Paperbag Studios; *Ink:* StazOn, Tsukineko; *Paint:* Making Memories, *Other:* Twill.

I compiled this 6" x 6" album to display some of Simon's art and work from kindergarten. This is the sort of book that's ongoing throughout the year. And I can easily add to it as the papers start to pile up on the kitchen counter. I kept it very simple and easy to maintain.

For this album, each piece is cropped and adhered to a thicker piece of cardstock for stability, then hole-punched. Don't be afraid to crop some of these gems—creative cropping can make each piece that much more visually interesting while maintaining the integrity of the artwork.

For the title page, I adhered lace cardstock behind a thick piece of acrylic. The lace cardstock and acrylic are sandwiched between two journaling cards. The front card introduces the concept of the book, and the second gives a bit more detail about what's inside the album.

KINDERGARTEN ART *by Ali Edwards.*
Supplies *Album:* American Crafts; *Patterned paper:* BasicGrey; *Initial accents:* Cosmo Cricket; *Transparency:* Hambly Studios; *Letter die-cut sheet:* KI Memories; *Letter journaling card:* Shim + Sons; *Rub-ons and word sticker:* 7gypsies; *"A" initial:* Jenni Bowlin Studio; *Font:* 1942 Report, Internet.

RECORD WHO YOU WERE AT A SPECIFIC MOMENT IN TIME

Create a record of a moment in time to share with your children and future generations. Laura created this 8" x 7½" book so she can give her future children a look into her life before they were born. "I know I love hearing stories from my parents about that time in their lives," Laura says. "I hope to pass our stories down to future generations."

Using a simple two-page formula, Laura used chipboard and rub-on letters and photo corners to create the left-hand side of each spread, then created a collage of images on the right-hand side to illustrate her journaling.

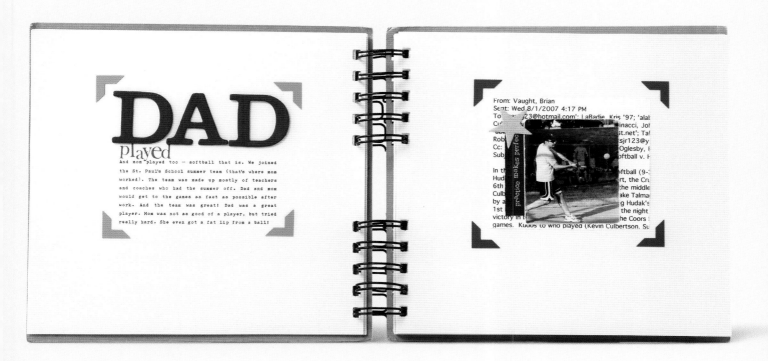

DAD
played

And mom played too — softball that is. We joined the St. Paul's School summer team (that's where mom worked). The team was made up mostly of teachers and coaches who had the summer off. Dad and mom would get to the games as fast as possible after work. And the team was great! Dad was a great player. Mom was not as good of a player, but tried really hard. She even got a fat lip from a ball!

From: Vaught, Brian
Sent: Wed 8/1/2007 4:17 PM
To: ...23@hotmail.com'; LaBadie, Kris '97'; 'alab...

practice makes perfec...

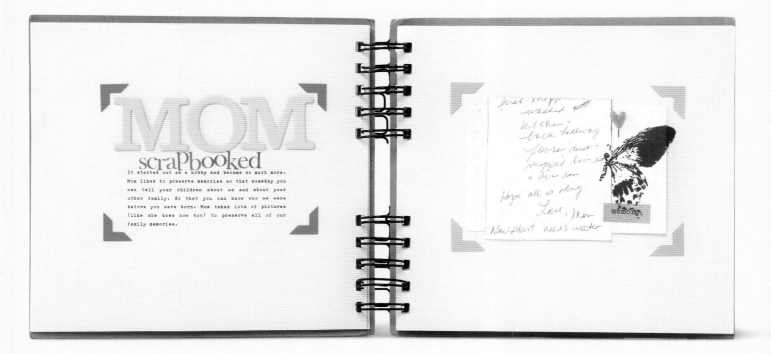

MOM
scrapbooked

It started out as a hobby and became so much more. Mom likes to preserve memories so that someday you can tell your children about us and about your other family. So that you can know who we were before you were born. Mom takes lots of pictures (like she does now too) to preserve all of our family memories.

memory

New plant needs water

BEFORE YOU *by Laura Kurz*

Supplies *Album:* 7gypsies; *Chipboard letters:* BasicGrey; *Photo corners:* American Crafts; *Rub-on letters:* Heidi Grace Designs; *Chipboard star:* Heidi Swapp for Advantus; *Pin:* Fancy Pants Designs; *Paint:* Making Memories; *Font:* Splendid 66, www.dafont.com.

37 ALL ABOUT ME
by Deena Wuest

CREATE A BOOK WITH A CHILD

Ever since Deena's seven-year-old daughter learned to write, she's loved writing about her favorite things and leaving notes and drawings throughout the house. Deena asked her to pick out some of her favorite photos and write a sentence about each one, then they created this 5" x 7" mini together. (*Note:* To create this digital project, Deena had her daughter write a sentence on plain white paper using a black marker and then scanned the handwriting and drawings.)

Says Deena, "I love that my daughter created this book on her own with a little help from me. And it not only holds her favorite photos, but also documents her handwriting and art."

Try This!

Use this mini for documenting:

- Another family member's experiences on a trip
- A holiday from a child's perspective
- Photos a child has taken

ALL ABOUT ME *by Deena Wuest.*
Supplies *Software:* Adobe Photoshop Elements 4.0, Adobe Systems; *Digital paper:* Purely Happy Paper Pack by Katie Pertiet, www.designerdigitals.com; *Cover template:* Tortuga Template No. 15 by Kellie Mize, www.designerdigitals.com; *Cardstock:* WorldWin; *Chipboard letters:* Rusty Pickle; *Ribbon:* C.M. Offray & Son; *Fonts:* Avant Garde and Impact, www.myfonts.com.

Soccer StaRs

a story
about
tyler
and
matthew
holmes

TELL THE STORY OF AN
EVENT IN STORYBOOK FASHION

A scrapbook or mini book is essentially the story of your life, so why not treat it like one? Here, Maggie told the story of her sons in a 6" x 6" mini titled "Soccer Stars." Says Maggie, "I created this book for my sons to showcase some of their pictures from soccer this year and to tell a story about them that they'll love to read over and over. Children love to read about themselves—who wouldn't want to be the star of a storybook!"

Try This!

Use this mini for documenting:

- A child's favorite bedtime story
- The first day of school or college
- The story of a new pet

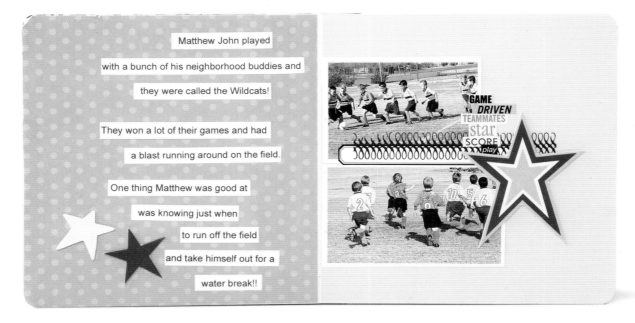

His favorite position to play was GOALIE!! He wanted to be the goalie every single game! He was really fabulous at stopping the ball and blocked it many times from entering the net!

coach BELIEVE compete RACE play

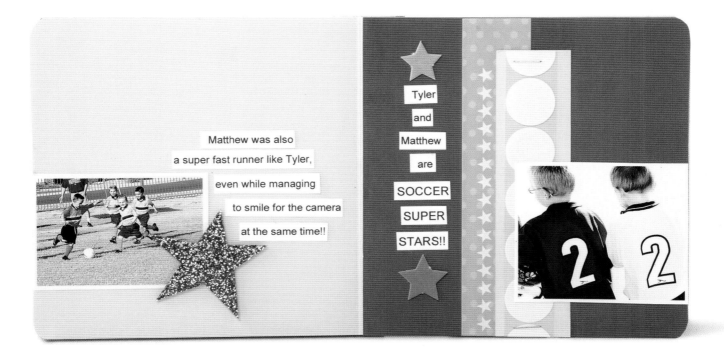

Matthew was also a super fast runner like Tyler, even while managing to smile for the camera at the same time!!

Tyler and Matthew are SOCCER SUPER STARS!!

SOCCER STARS *by Maggie Holmes*

Supplies *Album:* Cloud 9 Design, Fiskars; *Patterned paper:* My Mind's Eye, BasicGrey, CherryArte and Making Memories; *Transparency and rub-ons:* Hambly Studios; *Chipboard stars:* Making Memories, Scenic Route and Jenni Bowlin Studio; *Coaster stars:* Gin-X, Imagination Project; *Labels:* Li'l Davis Designs; *Word and letter stickers:* Making Memories; *Font:* Arial, Microsoft.

chapter 7

Travel

ONE OF MY FAVORITE WAYS TO BE CREATIVE WITH MINI BOOKS is to use them as travel journals. Capture the story behind your adventures, whether it's across town or across the globe. Tell the story of the first big vacation you took as a child or as an adult. Document where you go over the course of a week. Chronicle your adventures with photos, memorabilia and bits and pieces from your travels.

Or consider these ideas:

PHOTO-BASED TRAVEL JOURNAL. Using very few words and several pictures, record a trip through photos. Think of cool signs you saw on your trip or landscape shots or buildings or self-portraits of yourself on your adventure.

JOURNALING-BASED JOURNAL. Tap the writer within and share your experiences through words and anecdotes.

PERSPECTIVE JOURNAL. Work with a friend, child or partner to document your trip. We all see things differently—share that experience together.

Create a complete travel journal by combining travel photos with a collection of brochures, maps and postcards. You can easily incorporate photos and pamphlets of various sizes into your mini with binder rings. And flipping through the album will surely be a wonderful way to reflect on the journey for years to come.

"Travel albums are also great show-and-tell pieces for kids to bring to school," adds Maria Grace, who designed this practical 8" x 8" acrylic album to feature a variety of memorabilia from her trip. "These types of travel albums also work well as 'history books' for kids because they share personal photos of places they have likely only studied in books."

Try This!

Use this mini for documenting:

- An entire summer vacation
- A day trip to a museum
- A month of movie-going

CHEPSTOW, WALES *by Maria Grace Abuzman.*
Supplies *Overlays:* Hambly Studios; *Stamps:* FontWerks and Hero Arts; *Ink:* Ranger Industries and Tsukineko; *Foam stamps:* Kit of the Month, Creating Keepsakes; *Paint:* Blick; *Stickers:* Creative Imaginations, Heidi Grace Designs, Jenni Bowlin Studio, KI Memories, Scenic Route and Making Memories; *Rub-ons:* Autumn Leaves, Hambly Studios and Making Memories; *Journaling card:* Jenni Bowlin Studio; *Other:* Acrylic sheets, binder rings, clothing button, silver clip, shipping tag and ephemera from trip.

The Origin of the Welsh Lovespoon

The custom of giving lovespoons dates back as far as the early sixteenth century. It developed from the Cawl (soup) spoon, which young men would have been carving on a regular basis for use in the home. Traditionally they would have carved intricate designs into the handle of the wooden spoon to give to a young girl, hoping to begin a lifelong relationship.

These days lovespoons are given on special occasions, e.g. Engagements, Weddings, Anniversaries, Births, Birthdays, Christenings, Valentines or simply as a token of affection. They also make a wonderful memento of a visit to Wales.

Here are a few of the traditional symbols and their meanings:

Heart – for love, affection or friendship
Hearts entwined – love is returned
Bells – Engagements, Weddings and Anniversaries
Diamond Shape – for good fortune
Horseshoe – for good luck
Vines/trees – Grow together-full and fruitful
Chain links – for loyalty-faithfulness-life together forever
Flowers – for gentleness and growth
Ball in Cage – The number of children desired
Celtic Cross – faith and/or Wales
Lock – safekeeping or security
Shield – safekeeping
Birds – lovebirds
Welsh symbols – Dragon, Daffodil, Celtic Cross

my very first castle

These ladies were fantastic. So gracious and friendly, and such a pleasure to be with. This picture reminds me of the reason for my travels – to make a connection with others.

Before Emily went on vacation, she painted the pages of this 6" x 6" album and stamped a few journaling spaces so she could jot down notes during the trip. When she returned home, she printed and added her photos, along with other bits and pieces she collected while she was on the road. Says Emily, "It was great to have everything ready to create the album while the memories were fresh in my mind!"

Try This!

Use this mini for documenting:

- A road trip
- Summer camp
- A week of activities

NY by Emily Falconbridge

Supplies *Album:* BasicGrey; *Paint and gel medium:* Matisse Derivan; *Stamps:* FontWerks and Autumn Leaves; *Rub-ons:* Hambly Studios (gold), Autumn Leaves (white and black letters) and BasicGrey (paint splats and scroll frame); *Other:* Masking tape and ribbon.

Instead of a creating a typical travel scrapbook that records your impressions and memories, consider incorporating the perspectives of other family members. The beauty of involving children in this process is that it will help reinforce their memories of these childhood vacations. You can create journaling spots for them to write on or follow Mou's example and record their impressions through transcripts of your conversations with them.

In this 5¼" x 5¼" mini, Mou documented both her perspective and her daughter's. The pages of her album are actually tags that open up like flags facing two different ways, which also represents their two different points of view.

Try This!

Use this mini for documenting:

- Favorite quotes
- Family reunions
- The first day of school

Me: Nini, please stand still, I need to put the sunscreen on you.

U: Sunscream is VERY important. It keeps you from becoming a lobster.

THE FUTURE'S SO *Bright* IT BURNS MY EYES

I THOUGHT YOU PACKED IT...

BAYWATCH WANNABE

OUR FAVORITE BEACH
the one right behind the RESORT!

OFFICIAL BEACH BUM

WARNING EXTENDED BEACH EXPOSURE MAY RESULT IN DIFFICULTY RETURNING TO REALITY

OBSERVATIONS FAVORITES

Me: Wow! A waterfall! Such a pleasant surprise!

U: But it is not as good as the waterslide!!! Could we go back to the pool... rLeeeeease!

FINDERS KEEPERS MEMENTOS FINDERS KEEPERS

LAZY DAYS OF SUMMER MAY 14-21 2006 DATE LAZY DAYS OF SUMMER

LOOK WHAT I FOUND FOUND LOOK WHAT I FOUND

BIG BLUE

SAND

OUR BEACH VACATION by Maya Sakai

Supplies *Patterned paper:* 7gypsies (cover) and Frances Meyer (accordion spine and inside cover); *Large antiqued tags:* Rusty Pickle; *Cardstock stickers:* 7gypsies (tags), EK Success (on covers) and American Crafts (letters); *Chipboard sticker:* Heidi Swapp for Advantus; *Stamp:* Autumn Leaves and 7gypsies (time, place and dedication); *Braiding cords, beads and ribbon:* Michaels; *Drink umbrella:* Target; *Pens:* American Crafts (black) and Newell Rubbermaid (white).

The shade of an Oak on the other side of the world is worth visiting

Use this mini for documenting:

- Highlights of the year
- Alphabets, numbers or other educational tools for a child
- The special people in your life

CREATE AN EXPANDABLE JOURNAL TO HOLD YOUR TRAVEL MEMORABILIA

Paolo came up with the idea for an expandable travel book from a map he received at the airport in Amsterdam. "I wanted to use the same concept to document some of my travels, but I wanted to allow for an expanded perspective," he explains. "I love the versatility of the project—how it folds down to 7¾" x 5⅝", which is compact and easy to store, yet it expands to present an overview of all my travels."

Paolo designed this travel book with pockets to hold memorabilia, such as postcards and tickets, as well as photos and journaling in 12 equally divided sections. This expandable album is a fun and practical concept for almost any kind of theme—from documenting each month in a year to creating an educational project for a child that can be folded up for trips or hung on a bedroom wall.

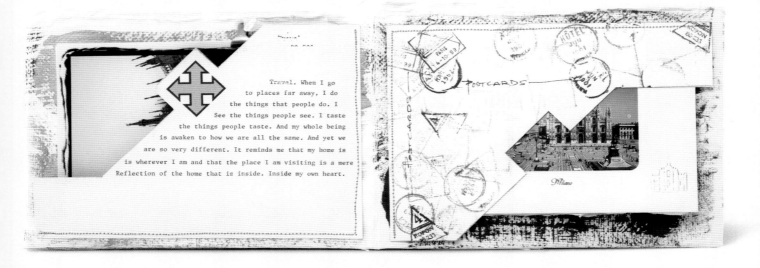

Travel. When I go to places far away, I do the things that people do. I See the things people see. I taste the things people taste. And my whole being is awaken to how we are all the same. And yet we are so very different. It reminds me that my home is is wherever I am and that the place I am visiting is a mere Reflection of the home that is inside. Inside my own heart.

TRAVEL TREASURES *by Paolo Liloc.*

Supplies *Software:* Adobe Photoshop CS3, Adobe Systems; *World map, handmade mulberry paper and lotus-print paper:* PaperZone; *Oak-tree image:* Jesuit Publication; *Translucent marker paper:* Bienfang; *Digital foliage brushes:* Japanese Foliage, *www.designfruit.com; School clip:* Karen Foster Design; *Fonts:* Scriptina (front cover) and Stamp Act (interior front cover), *www.1001freefonts.com; Other:* Chipboard, paint, mini-pocket sleeve, Egyptian foreign currency, and miscellaneous travel and museum tickets.

chapter 8

The Whole Story

AS YOU'VE PROBABLY GATHERED BY NOW, I'M BIG ON *TELLING THE STORY*. The idea of telling the *whole story* is really how I look at most minis. *Whole-story* minis often cover a span of time. Days, weeks, months or a lifetime. The "whole story" doesn't mean it has to have more words than any other mini—it just shares a more complete version of an event, time period or specific story. Very often, photos can tell a whole story all on their own.

Think about the stories you want your family to remember. Whether it's the story behind one event, like a family reunion, wedding or holiday celebration, or a compilation of memories, such as your teen years, a mini is the perfect way to chronicle it.

Try This!

Use this mini for documenting:

- Birthday activities or a party
- The first day at a new job
- A newborn's first week at home

It's no secret that I love scrapbooking everyday life. Documentation that tells the story over the course of an hour, a day, a week, a month or a year provides priceless insights into our lives. For this 4" x 6" album, I detailed three different times over the course of a day. I focused on the photos by using just a few words for a short description to embellish.

For the interior, I added a collection of transparent pieces (clocks and patterns) to reinforce my theme, intermixing them with photos glued back to back. Simply adhering photos back to back is one of my favorite ways to create pages for minis. For journaling, I wrote down a thought or two and adhered them directly to the photos.

TODAY *by Ali Edwards.*

Supplies *Album:* D. Reeves Design House; *Rub-ons:* 7gypsies; *Foam letter and number stickers:* American Crafts; *Transparencies:* Hambly Studios and Heidi Swapp for Advantus; *Chipboard circles:* Scenic Route; *Journaling blocks:* Heidi Swapp for Advantus; *Pen:* American Crafts.

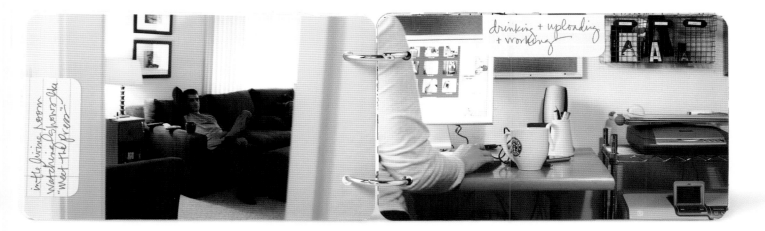

CELEBRATING TURKEY WEEK

44 *by Ali Edwards*

WEDNESDAY   THURSDAY   FRIDAY   SATURDAY
mcdougall + edwards + gitomer = celebrating turkey week 2007

This 6" x 6" mini celebrates the whole story of our weeklong Thanksgiving holiday. I used a variety of photos to document both the small and big events over the course of the week; words fill in a bit more of the details. This is Simon's favorite sort of book because he loves to identify the people and talk about his memories.

With these types of chipboard books, I often print my photos a bit larger than the page in the book, trim the photo down and adhere, then turn the page over on my scrapbook table and use a craft knife to remove the excess. For a unique cover, I used this turkey art project Simon made in school. (It just seemed to be the most appropriate choice!) To adhere it, I used a decoupage medium (such as Mod Podge) and then sealed it by applying more decoupage medium over the top.

Try This!

Use this mini for documenting:

- Everyone's favorite holiday activities
- All the photos you took on one day and why
- Activities for one season

CELEBRATING TURKEY WEEK *by Ali Edwards.*

Supplies *Album:* Cloud 9 Design, Fiskars; *Patterned paper, interior stickers and book-binding tape:* 7gypsies; *Journaling cards:* Jenni Bowlin Studio; *Turkey art:* Simon Edwards; *Stickers on first page:* Creative Café; Narratives, Creative Imaginations; *Pen:* American Crafts.

Family . You sat at the table for grace & that was about it — no interest in food (come to find out later ~ you were getting sick). Captured this one silly smile. And another favorite photo from this week: you + jess + jeffreys playing Ms. Pacman at a hole-in-the-wall in Charleston.

love

Your first time on a HORSE & talk about a cool way to wrap up a thanksgiving week. You ABSOLUTELY loved it.

★

RECORD ALL THE SPECIAL DETAILS ABOUT THOSE YOU LOVE

Maggie wanted to record her children's favorite things from the past year, including songs, movies and foods. "I wanted the album to be small and fairly simple, so I kept it to one photo for each child and a basic list of their favorite things," she shares.

To create her mini, Maggie cut an acrylic overlay to 3" x 5" for the front and back covers. She trimmed her photos to 3" x 5" and adhered them to the front of library cards. She used stickers to write each family member's name on the back of each card and then listed their favorite things for the year. To keep the mini safe and protected when it's not being viewed, she decorated a 3½" x 5½" library pocket and tucked the mini inside.

TYLER

color - red
sport - football
cookie - oatmeal raisin
food - doughnots
cereal - fruity pebbles
show - college football
movie - cars
song - once there was a snowman
thing to do - play video games
restaurant - chick-fil-A

WHAT WE LOVE *by Maggie Holmes.*

Supplies *Patterned paper:* My Mind's Eye and Making Memories; *Buttons:* Autumn Leaves; *Ribbon, shape die cuts and stickers:* Making Memories; *Library pocket:* Li'l Davis Designs; *Punch:* Fiskars; *Rub-ons:* Making Memories and Hambly Studios; *Transparency:* Hambly Studios; *Chipboard numbers, letters and letter stickers:* Heidi Swapp for Advantus; *Cardstock stickers:* Heidi Grace Designs; *Pen:* Zig Writer, EK Success; *Other:* Library cards.

MATTHEW

color - orange
sport - basketball
cookie - "pumpkin cooks"
food - green beans
cereal - koala crisp
show - backyardigans
movie - power rangers
song - twinkle twinkle
thing to do - ride bikes
restaurant - in-n-out burger

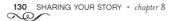

SHARE A HOBBY, INTEREST OR SPORTS PASSION

As a kid, I spent a good deal of time playing soccer. I wanted to remember and share this period in my life by creating an 8" x 6" mini to document the basic story as well as create a home for all the news clippings, photos and other memorabilia from my soccer days. To create the pocket for my patches, I stitched two 4" x 6" transparencies together, leaving the top open.

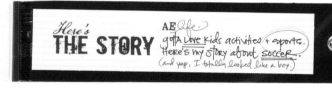

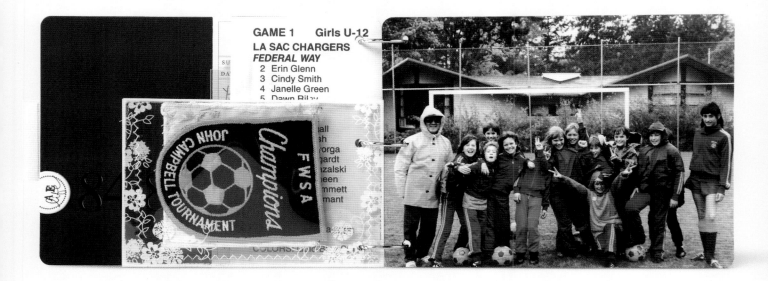

SOCCER *by Ali Edwards.*

Supplies *Album:* Cosmo Cricket; *Acrylic:* Hambly Studios; *Chipboard letters:* Heidi Swapp for Advantus; *Gold paint:* Ranger Industries; *Chipboard accents and number stickers:* Scenic Route; *Journaling cards:* Collage Press; *Transparencies:* My Mind's Eye; *Pens:* Sharpie (white), Newell Rubbermaid; American Crafts; *Other:* Stamps.

chapter 9

Personal Reflection

I LOVE SCRAPBOOKING MY PERSONAL STORY—IT'S A SIGNIFICANT PART OF MY BODY of work. You are really the only one who can tell your story with your own unique perspective. I can tell the story of my mom's life, but it would be so much more authentic and complete coming from her.

Over the last few years, I've noticed that scrapbookers find the smaller format of a mini book a more comfortable vehicle for telling their story. There's something about the size that makes it more accessible.

If you've never created a book about yourself (let alone a layout), now is the perfect opportunity. No day like today. Keep in mind that you don't have to share this mini until you're ready. Maybe during your lifetime . . . or maybe not. But taking the time to do it, to tell your story in your own words (from your own perspective), is quite a gift to future generations.

You
should
know

Use this mini for documenting:

- Tips and words of wisdom from family members to a new mom
- Welcome messages from a bride's new family
- A tribute to a loved one

SHARE THE UNIQUE DETAILS ABOUT EACH MEMBER OF YOUR FAMILY

This is one of my favorite books. I love it because it's rich with stories about the people in our family. The idea originally began when I thought about all the things Simon doesn't know about his grandparents, aunts and uncles, and even about me and my husband, Chris. So Chris and I sat down and came up with a bunch of tidbits about our family members and then invited them to contribute by e-mailing additional details about themselves.

For this 6½" x 6½" album, I really wanted to concentrate on the words and the photos, so one side of each spread is a photo and the facing page is entirely journaling. If your premade mini already has a spiral binding and you want your photos, journaling or patterned papers to run all the way to the edge of the page, you'll need to remove the binding first. (I'll share how to do this on page 158.) Otherwise, you can simply work with the album design by adhering your page elements just next to the edge of the binding.

YOU SHOULD KNOW
by Ali Edwards.

Supplies *Album and glass knob:* 7gypsies; *Patterned paper:* BasicGrey and Scenic Route; *Rub-ons:* Jenni Bowlin Studio; *Silver accent on first page:* 7gypsies; *Letter sticker:* American Crafts; *Font:* Garamond, Internet; *Other:* Words cut from old books.

CELEBRATE THE BLESSINGS IN YOUR DAILY LIFE

I love the idea of reflecting on and writing down something I'm thankful for each day. I've created many scrapbook layouts on the things I'm grateful for, too. But I really wanted something I could set on my nightstand or desk and add to each day—so I designed this simple 5½" x 8" daily gratitude journal. I created a simple template for each month with a line for each day.

When I began, I painted the cover of this mini with beige acrylic paint and added a rub-on date. I decided to change the color, so I added a coat of cream acrylic paint, allowing the rub-on to just barely show through the paint. Next, I punched various patterned papers using a circle punch and decoupaged them onto the cover to create the grid of 18 circles.

DAILY GRATITUDES *by Ali Edwards.*
Supplies *Album:* 7gypsies; *Patterned paper:* Taken from random bits of collected materials; *Circle punch:* Marvy Uchida; *Stamps:* Making Memories; *Ink:* StazOn, Tsukineko; *Paint:* Delta Creative; *Sealant:* Gel Medium, Blick; *Pens:* American Crafts and Newell Rubbermaid; *Fonts:* Marketing Script and Garamond, Internet.

Try This!

Use this mini for documenting:

- A relationship that changed your life
- Things you wish you knew about an ancestor
- Activities that define your relationship with people

TELL THE STORY OF A SPECIAL RELATIONSHIP

This mini documents my husband's relationship with his grandfather through stories about them hunting together. I decided to use one of my favorite mini formats—each spread has a photo on the left page and journaling on the right. This system is so efficient, yet it gives you the freedom to add different elements based on your theme.

The journaling in this mini is what I call "memories compilation." It's simply a grouping of one- or two-sentence snapshots of specific memories related to an event, person, etc. For this 7½" x 5" album, I printed the journaling on cardstock, then stamped and adhered additional elements, such as foam stickers for the age, initials for the first or last letter of a name, etc. Word stickers work great as well.

INTO THE WILD *by Ali Edwards*

Supplies *Album:* 7gypsies; *Cardstock:* Bazzill Basics Paper; *Clip:* Staples; *Transparency:* Narratives, Creative Imaginations; *Word stickers:* Making Memories; *Stamps:* Stamp-It and Cavallini & Co. (bird); *Ink:* Ranger Industries; *Rub-on:* Autumn Leaves; *Foam letter stickers:* American Crafts; *Ticket:* Jenni Bowlin Studio; *"R" accent:* Déjà Views, The C-Thru Ruler Co.

Did You Notice?

A basic design—for example, featuring a photo on one page and journaling and embellishments on the other—allows you to give both the photo and the story behind it equal treatment.

Try This!

Use this mini for recording:

· Your beliefs

· Your passions

· Lessons learned

SHARE YOUR LIFE'S PHILOSOPHY

Emily created this 4" x 5" accordion-style mini to share her philosophy and attitude toward life with her daughters. "There are so many things I want to teach my girls," she explains. "This is an ongoing project I can use to share life lessons from my experiences."

Emily wanted the album to be interactive so her daughters would enjoy the process of pulling out her notes from the pockets. To create it, she cut strips of fabric approximately 2" wide and slightly longer than the library pockets. Then she stitched one edge of the fabric to a library pocket, the other edge to a second library pocket and so on until she had sewn all the pockets together.

THIS I KNOW *by Emily Falconbridge.*
Supplies *Letter stickers:* Heidi Swapp for Advantus; *Rub-ons and chipboard tag:* Autumn Leaves; *Other:* Fabric, library pockets and a typewriter.

Try This!

Use this mini for documenting:

- Your values
- Achievements
- Your love for someone special

A mini can take any shape or form that best expresses who you are and what you want to say. Don't be afraid to experiment. Says Mou, "I created this mini book for myself using techniques I'd never tried before!"

Mou created this beautiful 7½" x 5½" handmade mini with fabric remnants and gorgeous decorative accents like beading and decorative pins. She journaled on twill strips by stamping letters with a solvent-based ink (try StazOn by Tsukineko). To create the foundation of her album, Mou used fabric remnants, chipboard and twill. She cut her fabric "pages" to size, then cut the chipboard pieces slightly smaller than the fabric to create solid page bases.

To construct the album, she worked in layers. First, she laid the bottom layer of fabric, placing the pieces down with the desired gaps in between. Next, she placed two twill ribbons (one close to the top and the other closer to the bottom of the fabric "page"), making sure to keep the ribbon long enough to tie the album closed at the end. She layered the chipboard pieces next (to give the fabric pages stability) and finally added the decorated fabric page on the top. Using some temporary adhesive to keep things in place, she carefully sewed each page border and twill binding in place. Once complete, the album folds up like an accordion—simply tie the loose ends of the twill to close!

MY GOALS *by Mou Saha.*

Supplies *Fabric remnants:* Jo-Ann Stores and Wal-Mart; *Lace, sewing pins and safety pins:* Jo-Ann Stores; *T-pins:* Staples; *Embroidery floss:* DMC; *Beads:* Michaels and Wal-Mart; *Letter stamps:* Martha Stewart Crafts and K&Company; *Ink:* Tsukineko; *Ribbon:* Michaels and Making Memories (velvet); *Silk flowers:* Prima; *Transparency bird:* My Mind's Eye; *Other:* Chipboard.

MY GOAL IS TO BECOME AN **ARTIST**

WHO CAN USE THE POWER OF ART TO HEAL · FULFILL QUESTION · ACCEPT & LEAVE A LEGACY FOR HER CHILDREN TO BE PROUD OF

· TARGET · PURPOSE · OBJECTIVE · INTENT ·

I AM DOOMED

TO AN ETERNITY

OF COMPULSIVE WORK

NO SET GOAL ACHIEVED SATISFIES

SUCCESS ONLY BREEDS A NEW GOAL

BETTE DAVIS.

reference

Getting Started

WHETHER YOU HAVE A STACK OF PHOTOS AND A SPECIFIC ANECDOTE TO SHARE OR you want to record daily family activities, a mini is the perfect way to document that story. So where do you begin? I'll share my process for creating a mini book and show you some of the basic mini types you can consider for your project.

THE CREATIVE PROCESS

As you begin this journey of sharing your story through a mini book, think of yourself as an author, designer and publisher. By the end of the process, you'll have transformed a blank book into your own personal work of art. Are you ready to start? It's easy. Let's go!

STEP 1: DECIDE ON YOUR THEME AND MINI SIZE.

What story do you want to tell? How many pages will you need to tell it? How many photos? Creating an outline, sketch or plan for yourself before you begin will make the entire process so much easier. Begin with the end in mind.

STEP 2: WRITE YOUR JOURNALING.

Writing out your journaling in advance, whether you use your computer or your own handwriting, will help you plan how much room you'll need for it. I often type the journaling in my minis. Part of the reason is that I can set up a template in a page-layout program, such as Adobe InDesign. This way, I can figure out exactly how large to make my font and how much space my journaling will take up. This makes it really easy for me to figure everything out before I print it onto cardstock, add it to the book and embellish.

STEP 3: GATHER YOUR MATERIALS.

Choose materials (patterned papers, accents, stamps, etc.) that match the theme of your book. Gather all of your photos and journaling.

STEP 4: ASSEMBLE YOUR FOUNDATION.

When creating a mini, I like to work in production mode, which feels most efficient for me. So I do my tasks in stages: I cut all the paper at once and adhere it to the pages, then I adhere all the photos, then add journaling, etc. Do what works best for you. Go with the flow. For some projects, it definitely makes more sense to work spread by spread; this is one of those choices to make before you begin.

STEP 5: EMBELLISH AS DESIRED.

If you'll be using your mini or filling it in on a regular basis, this step will be an ongoing process. Use lots of embellishments or just a few. Use several photos or no photos. A lot of journaling or a little. It's up to you.

TYPES OF MINI BOOKS

Part of the fun of creating a mini is choosing from the different types of blank premade books available. As you consider these options, think about what's important to you in a mini book. Do you want sturdy chipboard pages? A spiral binding? Pockets? Remember, you can always alter books according to your specific needs (for instance, adding pockets to pages or replacing binder rings with ribbon), so there's no limit to what you can create! Here's a quick look at some of the basic options.

Mini Cardstock Albums

Lightweight and compact, mini cardstock albums make great gift books—just add photos and embellishments. The flat size makes them ideal for sharing and even mailing as gifts.

Acrylic Albums

Bringing a new dimension to mini books, these popular albums feature clear covers and pages. The sheets are rigid enough to serve as page backgrounds but are thinner than chipboard. Acrylic albums, just like transparencies, are great for incorporating rubons and elements that layer well with the images and journaling on other pages.

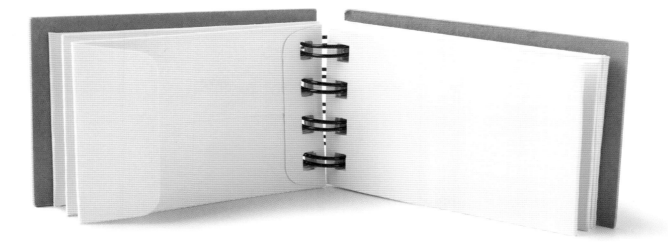

Tag/Envelope Albums

Pages in a mini can take many shapes and forms. Mini books with tag or envelope pages give you the flexibility for creative journaling and even adding interactive elements.

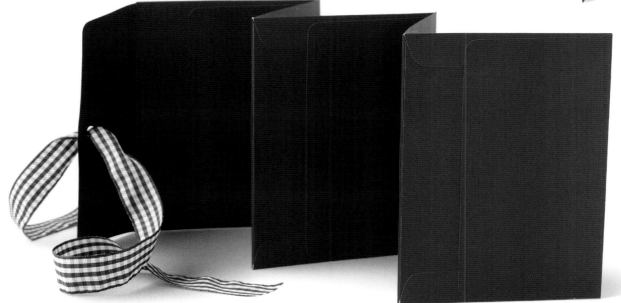

Chipboard Albums

The thickness of chipboard albums makes them ideal for minis for children or as table-top decor. Chipboard albums are typically kraft-colored but are also available in other colors, including black and white. Some chipboard albums have chipboard covers and interior pages, while others feature interior pages made of cardstock.

Accordion-Fold Albums

These compact minis are great for projects that don't require a lot of bulk. True to their name, these books expand like an accordion, with each page folding over the other to close. They're ideal for displaying open on a desk or shelf.

Mini Albums with Page Protectors

Just as with typical 12" x 12" albums with page protectors, you can also opt for mini albums with page protectors, available in sizes such as 9" x 9", 8" x 8" and 6" x 6". Create pages just as you would normally, except on a much smaller canvas . . . they're perfect for letting those 4" x 6" prints shine! Choose from a variety of bindings, including spiral, ring or post systems.

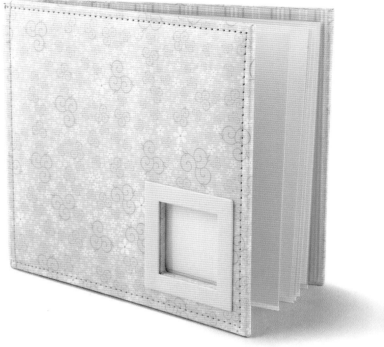

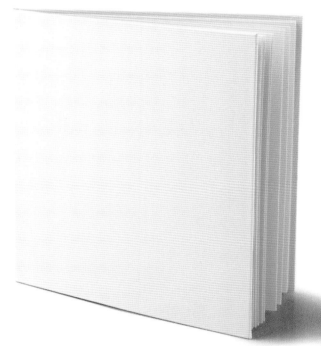

Hardbound Storybooks

A variant of chipboard albums, hardbound storybooks are designed like a typical children's hardcover book. These books are perfect bound (like a traditional book), rather than spiral bound.

Other Specialty Albums

As the popularity of minis continues to grow, so will your options. In addition to clear acrylic albums and chipboard storybook albums, you'll find specialty albums in a variety of styles, materials and textures, such as this blackboard album from Cosmo Cricket.

tips and solutions

Mini Books You Can Make

WHEN YOU'RE READY TO BEGIN A MINI BOOK, YOU'LL FIND MANY COOL PRODUCTS at your local craft or scrapbooking store, but you can also create a quick mini just by raiding your own stash of supplies! Create an easy gift mini or build a book project from scratch by starting with some basic supplies: cardstock, patterned or specialty papers, ribbon, adhesive and the binding (machine-stitching, staples, binder rings, etc.) of your choice!

Create a basic accordion-style book.

The beauty of the basic accordion-style mini? You get a whole lot of mileage out of one sheet of cardstock or patterned paper. Here's how:

1. Divide a sheet of cardstock in thirds. (You can use pencil marks to determine where your folds will be.) Make your first fold.

2. Fold the opposite edge.

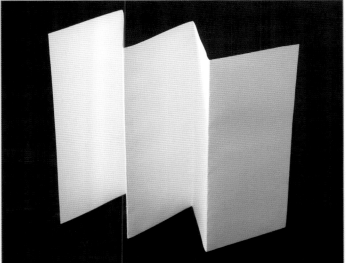

3. Add additional "pages" to your book by following the above steps to create another folded sheet, then adhere both sheets to each other. If desired, you can add chipboard to the front and back covers of your book for stability.

4. Embellish as desired.

Note: You can also fold the sheet in half first, then add other folds using the center fold as your guide. This will create a four-page accordion instead of a three-page accordion.

Make a mini stitched booklet.

Creating the base for a mini booklet is just one step beyond making a card. It's easy! Here's how:

1. Cut your cardstock and/or patterned paper to the desired size.

2. Score and fold each sheet.

3. Open the sheets and arrange them so the cover page is on the bottom of the stack. Stitch down the center of your stack.

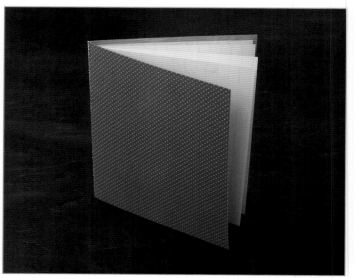

4. Embellish as desired.

Note: Experiment with different types of binding. For example, you can hand-stitch down the center instead of using a sewing machine or use a stapler.

Create a ribbon–bound mini.

If you want to create a mini book with the flexibility to add extra pages later, create an album with a ribbon or ring binding. Here's how:

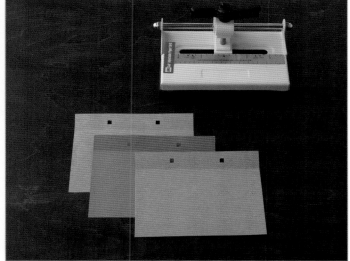

1. Cut your cardstock cover and interior pages to size. Score the sheets about ½" from the top (or side, depending on whether you want a top binding or side binding).

2. Use a pencil to mark where your binding holes will be. Add holes with a hole punch or paper drill.

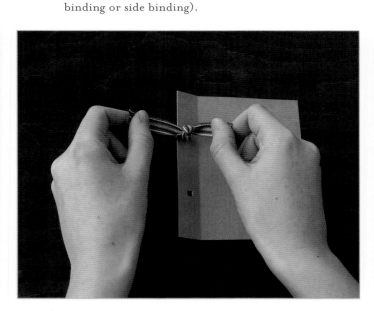

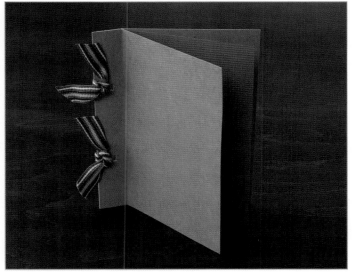

3. Bind your pages with ribbon. You can also use binder rings, prong fasteners, fabric strips, beaded-chain clasps and more. Experiment with different options to best match your album.

4. Embellish as desired.

From practical and functional spiral bindings to the handmade feel of ribbon and fabric bindings, your options for making a mini unique are many. Here's another look at some of the clever binding options showcased in this book:

Binder Rings

Binder rings are one of the easiest and most common methods of binding mini albums. Available at most office-supply stores, these secure fasteners offer plenty of flexibility. Adding pages is as simple as opening the rings and sliding more pages on. Use large binder rings for albums with several pages and small rings for minis with fewer pages.

Prong Fasteners

Most office-supply stores carry these standard fasteners. To create your own mini with cardstock and a prong fastener, simply use the fastener as a template to decide where to add holes to your cover and pages.

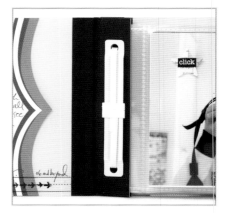

Spiral Binding

Many premade books already have spiral bindings. If you make your own book, you can have it professionally bound at most office-supply stores. Another option? If you plan to make several mini books, you can purchase a spiral-binding machine, such as Bind-it-All by Zutter Innovative Products.

Fabric Binding

Fabric remnants can add a soft touch to an accordion-style mini book. Use strips of fabric to connect each page. To close the album, simply fold each page as you would an accordion-style album. To add more pages, sew another page and strip of fabric to the last page of the album.

Plastic Zip-Ties

Any closure that's secure can work for your mini—even plastic zip-ties! Make sure to leave enough room before cutting off the excess plastic so you can easily turn pages, and remember to file down sharp edges on the plastic. You can also hang small charms or ribbon from the plastic binding.

Sewing

Machine-stitching along the center seam is a secure way to bind a mini, particularly if your pages or memorabilia items are different sizes. For minis with fewer pages, consider hand-stitching or stapling instead.

Design Basics

Q: I WANT TO GET STARTED, BUT I'M FEELING INTIMIDATED BY ALL THE CHOICES. ANY WORDS OF ADVICE?

A: Remember: Any premade book will work for the story you're sharing, so don't worry too much about the format. Instead, concentrate on what will work best for your story and the elements, such as memorabilia, you want to feature. Here are a few more ideas I like to keep in mind:

1. You can always create your own album. Grab some leftover chipboard and use it as the base of your album. Cover with photos or fabric or patterned paper.

2. Don't be afraid to remove excess pages from a premade album. You don't have to fill an album up just because that's how it came when you bought it. I often remove pages I just don't need.

3. I love to work with binder rings because I can add other elements (such as back-to-back photos) to create additional pages.

Q: HOW DO I CREATE A COHESIVE DESIGN FOR MY ALBUM?

A: Establish a design formula first. Draw out a sketch. Make a plan. For me, this always begins with what I want to say and then what I want to show. I create very basic design formulas and repeat them over and over. One of my favorites is a photo on one page and journaling on the opposite page. Regardless of the theme, this design always works for me.

Q: WHAT'S THE BEST WAY TO ADD DIFFERENT-SIZED PAGES TO MY ALBUM?

A: The easiest way is to simply cut pages to the same height as your base cover and vary the widths. Mini books are great because they're really open-ended in terms of what you can add as pages.

Gently pull them apart with your fingers—I usually end up using both hands.

2. Remove all the pages and the front and back covers. Normally, I take the entire book apart—this makes it easier to get at each of the pages and gives me more flexibility in my design. Put the binding aside in a safe place.

3. When I'm working on the interior pages, I tend to complete one side at a time, punching holes after covering each page. This way, I know where the holes are supposed to go when I create the page on the flip-side.

Note: Though the holes in spiral-bound books are typically rectangular, I usually just use a round hole punch. It doesn't bother me to have round holes instead of rectangles—eventually the round holes will become more like rectangles as the book relaxes with use. However, you do have other options, such as the border punch with rectangle holes by 7gypsies, the hand-held rectangle hole punch by Fiskars and the punch tool kit by Beary Patch. Go online or check your local scrapbook or craft store for similar options.

Q: I NOTICE YOU OFTEN DESIGN RIGHT UP TO THE EDGE OF THE PAGE ON SPIRAL-BOUND BOOKS. HOW DO I REMOVE THE SPIRAL BINDING SO I CAN DO THE SAME?

A: It takes a bit of extra effort to remove the binding, but it's not hard to do. Just follow these three steps:

1. Remove the spiral binding. To do this, open to the back page and locate where the spirals meet.

Q: I'VE TAKEN OFF THE SPIRAL BINDING OF A PREMADE BOOK TO DECORATE THE PAGES. NOW, HOW DO I PUT IT BACK ON?

A: After decorating you pages, put the spiral back in place following these steps:

1. Stack your pages in the correct order.

2. Move the back cover from the bottom of the stack and place it on the top, with the interior page facing up.

3. Run the spirals back through the holes so they meet in the inside of the book (between the last page and the back cover).

Journaling

Q: I'M NOT SURE HOW TO FIT EVERYTHING I WANT TO SAY. ANY ADVICE?

A: Plan this out in advance as part of your design formula. I often begin by typing up my story. Knowing what I want to say helps me plan the size, design and look of my mini.

Q: WHAT'S THE BEST WAY TO INCORPORATE COMMENTS FROM FRIENDS AND FAMILY MEMBERS IN MY MINI BOOK?

A: One of my favorite ways to include loved ones is to e-mail them and ask for contributions. I give them some guidelines and a deadline. Because their responses are already typed when I receive them, I simply copy and paste them into my project document. But consider including handwritten content, too—just give contributors specific directions and have them scan their messages or mail them to you.

Photos

Q: HOW DO I CROP MY PHOTOS TO FIT MY ALBUM?

A: Sometimes the best option when you're starting out is to choose a premade mini album designed for a specific photo size, such as 4" x 6" or wallet-sized prints. Otherwise, you can use a photo-editing program, like Adobe Photoshop or iPhoto, on your digital or scanned photos, or a punch or trimmer for your prints. In general, I measure my mini-book pages and print my photos the size of my book (most of my minis include page-sized photos).

Q: HOW DO I FIT MULTIPLE PHOTOS IN MY ALBUM?

A: One of my favorite ways to include a lot of photos is to create back-to-back photo pages—I simply adhere one photo to the back of another and add it to the binding of the book. You can also use a photo-editing program or a punch to create a mosaic or collage of photos that's the same size as your page. You can also add pockets to pages to hold additional photos.

Memorabilia

Q: SHOULD I WORRY ABOUT THE ARCHIVAL SAFETY OF TICKET STUBS AND OTHER MEMORABILIA? HOW DO I MAKE SURE THEY'RE SAFE?

A: It's completely up to you. If you're concerned about archival safety, use a deacidification spray on items like ticket stubs and newspaper clippings to neutralize the acids. Another great option is to scan or photograph the items instead of using the originals.

Q: ANY TIPS FOR SCANNING MEMORABILIA TO INCLUDE IN MINI ALBUMS?

A: Scan at 300 dpi for the best quality when printing. You can reduce the print size so scans will fit within a smaller book. Or leave your memorabilia as is and create pockets (or use premade pockets or envelopes) to hold it. Feel free to use larger albums to store items that are too big to include in a mini.

Displaying

Q: I WANT TO DISPLAY MY MINI BOOKS. ANY SUGGESTIONS?

A: I'm a big fan of storing minis out in the open for people to look through. Mine are currently sitting in a long basket on a bureau in our dining room. Other ideas?

- Stack them in large glass jars.
- Stash them in different areas around your home. Spread them out. Simon has a few on a shelf in his bedroom (usually they're whichever are his favorites at the moment).
- Pile them in locker baskets.
- Keep them inside photo boxes with lids (a dust-free storage option).
- Display a mini open on a cookbook holder or mini easel.